# THE NATIONAL GUARD

# THE NATIONAL GUARD

## An Illustrated History
## of America's
## Citizen-Soldiers

### Second Edition

## MICHAEL D. DOUBLER and JOHN W. LISTMAN JR.

### *Foreword by Donald M. Goldstein*

Potomac Books, Inc.
Washington, D.C.

**Library of Congress Cataloging-in-Publication Data**
Library of Congress Cataloging-in-Publication Data

Doubler, Michael D. (Michael Dale), 1955-
The National Guard : an illustrated history of Americas citizen-soldiers / Michael D. Doubler and John W. Listman Jr. ; foreword by Donald M. Goldstein. — 2nd ed.
p. cm.
Includes bibliographical references and index.
ISBN 978-1-57488-703-7 (pbk. : alk. paper)
1. United States—National Guard—History. I. Listman, John W. II. Title.
UA42.D6823 2007
355.3'70973—dc22
2006036402

ISBN-10: 1-57488-703-3
ISBN-13: 978-1-57488-703-7

(alk. paper)

Printed in the United States of America on acid-free paper that meets the American National Standards Institute Z39-48 Standard.

Potomac Books, Inc.
22841 Quicksilver Drive
Dulles, Virginia 20166

Second Edition

10 9 8 7 6 5 4 3 2 1

# CONTENTS

# FOREWORD

This is the eighth book in the Brassey's series *America Goes to War*. It is unique in that it is the first one that I have not had a direct hand in writing. The other seven volumes are listed in the front matter of this book. Another book in this series, by me and the late Harry J. Maihafer, titled *World War I: The Story and Photographs,* is forthcoming.

*The National Guard: An Illustrated History of America's Citizen-Soldiers, Second Edition* complements all the other books in the series because it is about the American way of war in general. Most of our major wars could not have been fought without the Guard and the reserves, and while many Regulars may not like it, the following ballad—sung to the tune of "My Bonnie Lies over the Ocean"—is as true today as it was at the time of the American Revolution:

> Oh, here's to the Regular Army,
> Oh, here's to their wonderful plan.
> They call out the Guard and reservist,
> Whenever they get in a jam.

Those visiting the cemeteries at Gettysburg, Vicksburg, and Arlington, as well as almost any other cemetery where America's soldiers are buried, will be struck by the numbers of National Guardsmen who fought and died for the country. In fact, the litany of the National Guard and its contributions is as strong in American military history as that of the Long Gray Line of West Point.

The history of war in America is the history of the citizen-soldier, a story that has often been neglected. In this book, Col. Michael D. Doubler, a twenty-three-year veteran as a Regular Army officer and a full-time National Guard officer, and CW2 John W. Listman Jr., another veteran of twenty-two years of combined active duty and National Guard service, join forces to finally give the National Guard its due.

This book covers the period from 1607 to 2002 and is full of vignettes and illustrations, many never before published, of the rich history of the Guard. As the director of the Matthew B. Ridgway Center for International Security at the University of Pittsburgh and one who trains many future soldiers going into combat, I am constantly getting messages from former students, in places like Kosovo and Afghanistan, who remind me of the role of the Guard in today's military, which is just as vital today as it was 200 years ago. The following quote from an American soldier in Afghanistan is a good example:

> There are lots of problems getting people where they need to go; part of the problem is lack of cargo planes and pilots. We would be totally screwed without the Air National Guard who are actually doing most of the lifting of supplies. (A January 22, 2002, e-mail from the front)

In this book, I believe that Michael Doubler and John Listman have done an admirable job in telling the story of the National Guard and the citizen-soldier, with illustrations and text that clearly demonstrate the importance of their role in American military history.

On behalf of my colleagues, Mike Wenger, Katherine Dillon, and Harry Maihafer, who saw the book before he died, we are proud to have this book as part of our series. Besides adding a new dimension to the series, we believe that it will make an important contribution in depicting the role of the forgotten soldier—the men and women of the National Guard and citizen-soldiers—in American military history.

Donald M. Goldstein, Ph.D.
Professor of International and Public Affairs
University of Pittsburgh
Pittsburgh, Pennsylvania

# ACKNOWLEDGMENTS

The completion of an illustrated history of such a long-serving institution as the U.S. National Guard would not have been possible without the cooperation and interest of many organizations and individuals.

First, the National Guard Association of the United States in Washington, D.C., and its subsidiary institution, the National Guard Educational Foundation, allowed free access to its archival holdings and generously granted permission to use a large number of photographs that vividly portray the history of the Army and Air National Guard since 1945. The National Guard Bureau in Arlington, Virginia, and especially the Historical Services Division, provided expertise in finding the best photos to illustrate key aspects of the Guard's overall history. The National Archives and Records Administration in College Park, Maryland, made available numerous images that document the National Guard's history through 1953. The U.S. Army Military History Institute at Carlisle Barracks, Pennsylvania, provided a large number of images that illustrate the service of citizen-soldiers in the nineteenth century, especially during the American Civil War. The Anne S. K. Brown Military Collection at Brown University in Providence, Rhode Island, is a treasure trove of images related to the early militia. Lastly, National Guard organizations in a number of states freely offered the use of images related to the history of their citizen-soldiers and -airmen.

In addition to the aforementioned institutions, a number of individuals lent their expertise and granted permission to print key images. Dr. Charles J. Gross, a recognized expert on the history of the Air National Guard, graciously reviewed portions of the manuscript. Col. Leonid Kondratiuk (Ret.) provided open access to the holdings of the Massachusetts Military Museum and Archive and gave sage advice throughout the project. Capt. Doug Hartmann of the Nebraska National Guard gladly supplied a number of key photographs. In addition, a great number of individuals and institutions provided single images and helpful hints along the way. While too numerous to list here singly, their names appear in the photo credits. Lastly, Don McKeon and the thoroughly professional staff at Potomac Books were invaluable in designing the book and bringing the project to its completion.

Michael D. Doubler          John W. Listman Jr.
Col., ARNGUS (Ret.)         CW2, VA ARNG (Ret.)
Alexandria, Virginia        Alexandria, Virginia

# INTRODUCTION —————————————————————

The National Guard has had an enduring and powerful influence on America's development and eventual rise as a world power. When the first English settlers established their colonies in the New World, they brought to America the desires for freedom of speech, freedom of religious expression, the gaining of economic prosperity, and the defense of their lives and property. At the beginning of the twenty-first century, American society's major concerns have changed little. Over the past 400 years, the militia tradition ranks with the free press, freedom of religion, and private enterprise as institutions that have had a lasting and profound effect on our society.

In 2002, the National Guard consisted of nearly 450,000 men and women serving voluntarily in the Army and Air National Guard while stationed in the fifty-four states and territories that stretch from the U.S. Virgin Islands to Guam. Perhaps the most unique aspect of the National Guard is that it exists as both a federal and a state force. As a federal force, the Guard provides ready, trained units as an integral part of America's field forces. In its state role, the National Guard protects life and property and preserves peace, order, and public safety under the direction of state and federal authorities. No other reserve military force in the world has such an arrangement, and the National Guard's dual allegiance to state and nation has often been the subject of much controversy and misunderstanding. The National Guard stands separate and distinct from the other federal reserve forces of the Army, Navy, Air Force, and Marines. National Guard troops serve at the direction of the state governors until the president of the United States orders them to active duty for either domestic emergencies or overseas service. Still, National Guard men and women work in conjunction with full-time forces and the other federal reserves of the U.S. Army and the Air Force.

Rooted in the English tradition of militia service and firmly established by the U.S. Constitution, the composition and service of the National Guard has evolved in three distinct phases during the past 400 years. From its early beginnings in North America, the militia provided local protection and law enforcement and served as the basis for more ambitious military ventures. During the American Revolution, the militia fought the war's first battles, provided the foundation for the creation of the Continental Army, and contributed troop units of varying quality for a wide range of missions. Throughout the nineteenth century, militiamen enforced federal, state, and local laws; helped to create the vast, volunteer armies of the American Civil War; and protected settlers during westward expansion. In the aftermath of the Spanish-American War, the long era of militia service surrendered to the rise of the National Guard. With the Militia Act of 1903, the National Guard became the organized, trained, and equipped federal reserve of the U.S. Army. In two world wars, the National Guard proved its worth during battles in Western Europe and the Mediterranean basin and throughout the far-flung archipelagoes of the Pacific Ocean. After World War II, the modern Army and Air National Guard emerged as a bulwark against communist expansion. During the Cold War, National Guard citizen-soldiers deployed to East Asia, Europe, and Central America to help contain communism. After the fall of the Berlin Wall in 1989, National Guard soldiers and airmen ventured to Southwest Asia and the Balkans to implement a new national security strategy. Since the horrendous events of September 11, 2001, the National Guard has participated fully in the war on terrorism.

While much has changed since the creation of America's first citizen-soldier regiments in 1636, a number of the National Guard's important characteristics have remained constant. The National Guard has maintained its unique status as both a federal and state force. Another constant has been the dedication and service of its members. Since the demise of compulsory militia service in the 1840s, militia and National Guard soldiers have been volunteers all, willing to make the necessary sacrifices in their personal and professional lives to learn and maintain required military skills. From the earliest militia engagements in the New World to the National Guard's current role in the war on terrorism, Guard volunteers have performed exemplary, selfless service for both community and country. The National Guard has always been a community-based force, with citizen-soldier camps and armories appearing wherever the American people have ventured. At the same time, the National Guard has been a dynamic institution capable of responding to the nation's changing needs. From the musket to the microprocessor, Guard soldiers and airmen have quickly adapted to the new weapons and tactics of warfare.

In nearly four centuries, American militiamen have transformed themselves from a loose collection of local defense forces to a modern and ready U.S. National Guard that is perhaps the best reserve force in the world. While major policy decisions have made that transformation possible, the physical appearance of citizen-soldiers dramatically reflects the many changes that have occurred. In their uniforms, weapons, equipment, tactics and missions, the men and women of the National Guard have repeatedly cast aside outmoded means in favor of newer and more effective resources. The photos and illustrations on the following pages vividly portray that transformation.

# ABBREVIATIONS

| | |
|---|---|
| AAF | Army Air Forces |
| AEF | American Expeditionary Forces |
| AG | Adjutant General |
| ANG | Air National Guard |
| ARNG | Army National Guard |
| CNGB | Chief, National Guard Bureau |
| CONUS | Continental United States |
| DISCOM | Division Support Command |
| DOD | Department of Defense |
| HHB | Headquarters and Headquarters Battery |
| HHC | Headquarters and Headquarters Company |
| JCS | Joint Chiefs of Staff |
| JFHQ | Joint Force Headquarters |
| MP | Military Police |
| NATO | North Atlantic Treaty Organization |
| NGB | National Guard Bureau |
| NGAUS | National Guard Association of the United States |
| NTC | National Training Center |
| OEF | Operation Enduring Freedom |
| OIF | Operation Iraqi Freedom |
| PJ | Pararescueman |
| ROTC | Reserve Officer Training Corps |
| SF | Special Forces |
| SRF | Selected Reserve Force |
| UN | United Nations |
| USAF | United States Air Force |

## Public Repositories

| | |
|---|---|
| BROWN | Anne S. K. Brown Military Collection |
| CMH | U.S. Army Center of Military History, Army Art Collection |
| LC | Library of Congress |
| MEADE | Ft. George G. Meade Museum |
| MHI | U.S. Army Military History Institute |
| NASA | National Aeronautics and Space Administration |

| NARA | National Archives and Records Administration |
| NGB | Historical Services Division |
| NGEF | National Guard Educational Foundation |
| NPS | National Park Service |

## Commercial Repositories

| AUSA | Association of the U.S. Army |
| | Photos by Dennis Steele, *ARMY* magazine, copyright 2005, AUSA, used with permission |
| KENT | Special Collections, Kent State University Library |
| VHS | Virginia Historical Society |
| WSHS | Washington State Historical Society |

## State-Based Collections

| CANG | California National Guard Public Affairs |
| DCNG | District of Columbia National Guard Public Affairs |
| ILNG | Illinois State Military Museum |
| KSNG | Kansas National Guard History Museum |
| MDNG | Maryland National Guard Historical Collection |
| MAMM | Massachusetts National Guard Military Museum |
| NENG | Nebraska National Guard Historical Collection |
| PANG | Pennsylvania Air National Guard, 193rd Special Operations Wing |
| TXMM | Texas National Guard Military Museum |
| VTNG | Vermont National Guard Public Affairs |
| VANG | Virginia National Guard Historical Collection |

## Private Collections

| DOUBLER | Col. Michael Doubler (Ret.) |
| KACMARCIK | Mr. Michael J. Kacmarcik |
| LISTMAN | CW2 John W. Listman Jr. (Ret.) |
| PERKINS | Col. Donald Perkins (Ret.) |
| THOMPSON | Col. Gillard Thompson Jr. (Ret.) |

# ONE
# The Enrolled Militia, 1607–1794

## Early Militia Origins

In Western civilization, the concept of an armed citizenry finds its beginnings in ancient Greece. The Greek city-states required military service of all able-bodied, free male citizens. Such service was usually of short duration, and Greek citizen-soldiers fought locally to defend their own lands and city-state. The Romans adopted the concept of the citizen-soldier across their far-flung empire, and the word "militia" comes from the Latin term "miles," meaning "soldier."

After the fall of the Roman Empire, the militia concept endured through the Middle Ages as the Saxon fyrd that eventually took root in England. The Anglo-Saxon fyrd embodied two key concepts: each male was obligated to military service and citizen-soldiers had to provide their own arms and equipment. The real value of the fyrd was its ability to mass a great number of armed citizens at critical points on short notice. In the "Assize of Arms" promulgated in 1181, King Henry II of England formally levied the military obligation of every adult male in defense of the realm. Citizen-soldiers were required to arm and equip them-

selves based on their social status and economic standing. The Assize of Arms represented a turning point in the history of governments levying military obligations upon these soldiers.

Subsequent English laws provided better definition of the militia's characteristics. All males between fifteen and sixty years of age were enrolled in the militia and required to maintain arms. Musters were held twice annually, and wealthier individuals were required to provide the resources for those too poor to arm and equip themselves. Each shire appointed a "Lord Lieutenant," who was responsible for mustering the local militia, inspecting arms and equipment, and conducting periodic training. During Queen Elizabeth's long reign (1558–1603) "trained-bands," or trainbands, appeared. They represented a select group of militiamen chosen from each shire to receive proper arms and training. By 1583, 12,000 men out of the 180,000 carried on English muster roles were members of trainbands. Queen Elizabeth called out the trainbands in the summer of 1588 as the Spanish Armada approached the British Isles.

## America's First Citizen-Soldiers

The Spanish were the first to introduce European military institutions to the New World. On the heels of Columbus, Spanish conquistadores rushed to the New World in search of unimaginable riches. At the time of America's discovery, the powerful Aztec and Inca Empires ruled Mexico and South America. Though the Spanish brought new arms and tactics to bear against the Native Americans, communicable diseases wrought the most devastation; only one million Native Americans are believed to have survived into the seventeenth century.

The mining of vast deposits of gold and silver dominated Spanish interests. Regulars and citizen-soldiers protected the mines, controlled the Indian populations, and protected vital sea routes that allowed convoys to carry precious metals back to Spain. Spanish military bases developed in Panama and at Veracruz, Havana, and Santiago. In 1509 Spanish settlers founded San Juan on the island of Puerto Rico, organized themselves into militia commands, and successfully subdued the island's Caribbean Indians.

1-1 The Castillo de San Marcos at St. Augustine, FL, was constructed in the late seventeenth century in place of the original fort built in the 1580s. NGEF

1-2 The State Headquarters patch of the Florida National Guard bears the image of the Castillo as seen from above. NGEF

In September 1565 the Spanish established St. Augustine, the oldest permanent European settlement on the North American continent. Florida became a Spanish military province, with St. Augustine as its presidio, or headquarters. Soon after its founding, the Spanish commander designated St. Augustine's civilian settlers as *milicia* and made them responsible for defending the outpost while Spanish Regulars defeated nearby French ventures. Despite Indian uprisings and devastating raids from English privateers, St. Augustine survived as Spain's permanent outpost in North America. (See figures 1-1 and 1-2.)

While the Spanish gained control of Florida, the French soon occupied the St. Lawrence River valley and established a strong outpost at Quebec. In response to the serious threat posed by Native Americans, France committed Regular troops to the St. Lawrence valley and organized the local population for defense. Militia companies soon formed in New France. By the mid-1600s, French ministers at Versailles viewed a militarized Canada as the best means of containing the expansion of English settlements beyond the Appalachian Mountains.

Increasingly, England's attention turned toward opportunities in the New World. In late April 1607, a small English flotilla entered the Chesapeake Bay searching for a suitable site for a permanent settlement. The colonists were fully aware of the dangers from the Indians, Spanish, and French, and knew that their survival depended on their own abilities. The only means of defense for the 100 settlers was to fight as citizen-soldiers based on the English militia system.

On May 14, 1607, the English unloaded their vessels and established the Jamestown colony on the banks of the James River. Before long, Native Americans decided to eliminate the intruders, and 200 Indian braves assaulted the settlement. A sharp engagement followed in which two colonists died, the first English citizen-soldiers to die in America. In response, Jamestown became a fortified camp. Within a week, the colonists built a sturdy fort. The constant carrying of weapons became customary, day and night watches were established, and organized training on Saturday became an established routine. Though secure behind their defensive barrier, the settlers barely survived the ensuing winter. In September 1608 Capt. John Smith became Jamestown's undisputed leader. (See figure 1-3.) A mercenary by trade, he imposed discipline and training in order to guarantee the settlement's survival.

By modern standards, early militia weapons were extremely

1-3 Capt. John Smith was the military leader of the Jamestown Colony from 1608 to 1609. His memoirs were published in several English and German editions. VHS

1-4 An illustration of a Dutch pike officer, 1608. His armor and weapons are the same as those used by the early English colonists. BROWN

1-5 A musketeer armed with a matchlock from a 1608 Dutch print. BROWN

crude. Troops frequently wore metal helmets and various pieces of body armor, including breast- and back plates. Nearly one-third of these citizen-soldiers carried pikes, while others were armed with matchlocks, a dangerous and inaccurate gunpowder weapon. On muster days militiamen practiced the complicated tactics and techniques of European warfare. One commonly used drill book described fifty-six steps for loading and firing a matchlock. In addition, the troops armed themselves with an array of knives and hatchets, while leaders carried swords. (See figures 1-4 and 1-5.)

Captain Smith soon launched a series of devastating raids against the Native Americans. By the summer of 1609, Smith's offensive had resulted in an uneasy peace between Jamestown and local Native Americans. Weeks later, an exploding powder charge badly burned John Smith, and he returned to England for treatment. Unfortunately, expanding English settlements and efforts to convert the Indians to Christianity caused a widening gulf between the two peoples. On March 22, 1622, the Indians launched a massive, surprise attack against all English settlements along the James River. (See figure 1-6.) In one awful day of bloody attacks, the Native Americans killed 300 settlers. After recovering from the shock, the colonists launched a series of bloody reprisals. Additional arms came from England, and for the first time, widely dispersed plantations and farms included an armed citizenry. All males between the ages of sixteen and sixty were liable for militia duty, and the legislators levied a series of taxes to buy arms and equipment. By the 1630s Virginia mustered over 2,000 militiamen.

Meanwhile, 100 Pilgrims had established the Plymouth Colony on November 11, 1620. The Pilgrims had hired Capt. Miles Standish to act as a military adviser. Standish moved quickly to organize the Plymouth militia into four squadrons and instituted a thorough plan for watches, guards, and alarms. (See figure 1-7.) In late 1621 the Pilgrims conducted a militia muster as part of the first Thanksgiving celebration. By 1639 the expanding Plymouth Colony included eight militia companies in as many towns.

The Puritans of the Massachusetts Bay Colony took military matters very seriously. After the arrival of a large Puritan fleet in 1630, settlements quickly sprang up along the coast. As the population increased and spread inland, the Massachusetts General Court authorized militia companies, and by 1636 the colony included ten companies of approximately sixty men each. A captain commanded a company and had the responsibility for musters, training, and discipline.

On December 13, 1636, the Massachusetts General Court directed the establishment of the first militia regiments in North America. A total of fifteen separate towns contributed as many companies, with a combined strength of approximately 1,500 men to form three new regiments. Because Massachusetts was the first government in North America to raise militia regiments, December 13, 1636, is recognized as the birth date of the modern U.S. National Guard. (See figure 1-8.)

New England militiamen had their first, serious test in the Pequot War of 1637, from which they emerged victorious. The certainty of further Native American conflicts resulted in the creation of the American minuteman. To guarantee rapid responses against Native

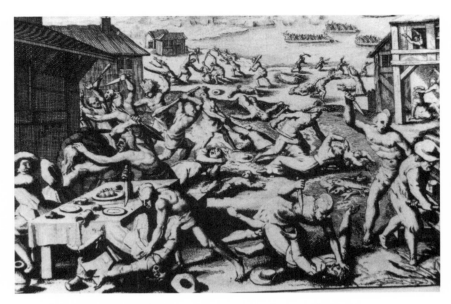

1-6 The "Massacre of 1622" caught the Virginia colony unprepared. However, during the following ten-year struggle, the militia became very proficient in raids and small-unit actions. VANG

1-7 "The March of Miles Standish" from an 1873 lithograph that portrays the militia in the Plymouth colony. BROWN

American raids, Massachusetts directed that a portion of the militia remain in a near constant state of heightened readiness. Each militia company was to select one-third of its members to respond to alarms within thirty minutes. Minutemen were to have their arms, ammuni-tion, and equipment ready for immediate use day or night.

In the aftermath of the Pequot War, Connecticut, Rhode Island, and New Hampshire created formal militia organizations. King Philip's War erupted in New England in 1675 and threatened the very

1-8 A diorama depicting the first muster of Massachusetts's newly organized regiments in 1637. NGEF

1-9 Virginia governor Sir William Berkeley appoints Francis Bacon as "generall and commander in cheife" of the militia with instructions to lead his troops against hostile Indians in 1676. Soon the two men led forces against each other in "Bacon's Rebellion." VANG

defense of the colonies, broken the power of the New England Native American tribes, and gained the long-term security of the region's white settlements.

## The Militia Expands and Evolves

In the decades following the first English settlements, all but one of the original thirteen colonies stretching from New Hampshire to Georgia established militia organizations. In Pennsylvania, the pacifist influence of the Quakers and peaceful relations with the Native Americans precluded the establishment of a militia until the middle 1700s. The militia included all men between the ages of sixteen and sixty enrolled for training and service at the local level. The militia system served as both a training base and a reservoir of manpower. Citizen-soldiers carried on muster rolls and formed into geographically based units available for immediate service during short-term emergencies became known as the enrolled militia. Militiamen provided their own weapons and equipment and elected their own junior leaders; governors appointed the most senior officers. (See figure 1-9.)

The early militia expanded and developed in a number of different ways. The quality of the militia varied greatly depending on the proximity of an immediate threat. When danger neared, colonial leaders energized the militia, but as threats evaporated,

existence of English settlements. As many as 1,000 settlers were killed, and Native American losses were perhaps much higher. The war effectively ended in August 1676,

when militiamen captured and executed a principal Native American chieftain. The most significant outcome of the war was that the militia had provided an adequate

units often fell apart from neglect. In New England, a society based on separate towns resulted in a militia system concentrated in closely knit, rural communities. In the South, economics and agriculture produced a plantation system that created militia units that were more widely dispersed, based on counties rather than towns, and concerned more often than not with the control of slave populations. (See figure 1-10.)

As settlements moved further inland, the Native American threat to seaboard communities waned, and the enrolled militia deteriorated. However, on the frontier, defense was still paramount. Settlers based their defenses on widely dispersed blockhouses and stockades manned by militiamen to provide protection against Native American uprisings. (See figure 1-11.) Militia ranger units patrolled the frontier hoping to detect or foil Native American attacks before they hit settlements. (See figure 1-12.) All along the forward face of the Appalachians, the colonies developed their own systems of forts and defense forces.

**1-10 Infantry and cavalry units of the New York militia pass in review before the governor in 1700. BROWN**

**1-12 Experienced backwoodsmen, known as "rangers," patrolled the frontier to give early warning of Indian attack. VANG**

**1-11 A frontier blockhouse, c 1750. NARA**

In the early 1700s, conflicting English, French, and Spanish interests involved the colonies in a series of near-continuous wars. The typical colonial war pitted the American colonies against the French Canadians with Native American allies on both sides. When ambitious expeditions required more than the militia's local, defensive capabilities, the colonies relied on ad hoc organizations known as "provincial" troops for extended military operations beyond their borders. Provincial units were formed from volunteers, draftees, substitutes, and hirelings who came from the enrolled militia.

The greatest use of militia provincial troops occurred during the French and Indian War of 1754–63 when England and France battled for domination in North America. To help guarantee success in America, Great Britain committed British Regulars to the fight. At the war's conclusion, British influence reigned supreme in North America. However, the battlefield performance of British Regulars and American militiamen was often mixed. George Washington emerged as the most successful colonial leader of the war.

Despite the war's successful outcome, British Regulars and colonial troops developed a loathing for one another. British officers considered the American colonists to be ill-disciplined, prone to desertion, and lacking in basic military skills. Convinced of the

## George Washington: Colonial Militiaman

George Washington received his first experience as a military leader while serving as an officer in the Virginia militia. In February 1753 the twenty-one-year-old Washington received the rank of major and a share of the responsibility for training Virginia troops. Ten months later he volunteered for active service against French incursions in the upper Ohio Valley.

Washington's service in the French and Indian War gained him widespread recognition and valuable experience. His first command resulted in a humiliating surrender that only further strengthened Washington's resolve. In 1755 he served as an aide to Maj. Gen. Edward Braddock during the disastrous British expedition against Fort Duquesne. Washington's display of raw courage and tactical skills during Braddock's Defeat caused his personal reputation to soar. Afterward, he assumed overall command of Virginia's frontier defenses. By 1758 Washington served as a brigade commander, the only American militia officer to achieve such rank in the war.

With the approach of the American Revolution, Washington accepted the command of the Virginia militia with the rank of colonel and represented the colony in the Continental Congress. After Lexington and Concord, the Congress appointed him to various committees dealing with military matters. On June 15, 1775, the Continental Congress unanimously elected Washington "General and Commander in Chief" of all Continental forces. For the next eight years, Washington led the Continental Army in battle and served as the Revolution's senior military officer while employing skills he first learned as a colonial militiaman.

limited aptitude of American troops, the British relegated most of them to support and auxiliary functions. Altogether, the British Army formed a low opinion of Americans as fighters, and it labeled the entire militia as an ineffective institution. Most British officers confused ad hoc provincial forces with the enrolled militia and consequently mis-

judged the militia's ability to respond to crises closer to home.

If British Regulars formed a low opinion of colonial troops, the converse was true as well. The quartering of British troops in colonial homes outraged Americans, who insisted the practice was illegal. Still, British authorities pointed to the exigencies of war and routinely placed troops in

**1-13 Col. George Washington of the 1st Virginia Regiment, 1772. BROWN**

American homes. The flogging of Redcoats for minor offenses appalled the colonists and further marked the British Army as a threatening and repressive institution. By the end of the French and Indian War, American citizen-soldiers held a high opinion of their own military prowess and a jaundiced view of the Regulars. The contempt that colonial militiamen held for British soldiers helped to lay the groundwork for an American uprising against Great Britain.

## The American Revolution

Great Britain established policies after the French and Indian War that eventually led to the American Revolution. The British Army remained in America after 1763 to protect the frontiers of the newly acquired territories, to maintain peace between settlers and Native Americans, and to regulate the fur trade. Many Americans were suspicious of a standing army posted on their land and argued that for nearly 150 years the enrolled militia alone had provided adequate security. Lastly, the British government for the first time instituted a series of colonial taxes designed to reduce its war debts and to pay the costs of maintaining Regular regiments in the colonies. Sensational events like the Boston Massacre in 1770 and the Boston Tea Party three years later further alienated Great Britain and the colonies.

The strong British response to American civil disobedience prompted colonial political leaders to convene a Continental Congress that encouraged the colonies to strengthen their militias. In Massachusetts, the colonists moved quickly to organize for self-defense. An intricate system of alarms and mounted messengers was created to facilitate quick, emergency communications across the countryside and to warn of unexpected British actions. The colony resurrected the minuteman concept, and minuteman companies were put on high alert. Aware of the colonists' activities and concerned over increasing American military power, British troops in Boston conducted a series of raids into the surrounding countryside starting in September 1774 to seize colonial arms, gunpowder, and war supplies.

The largest raid occurred on April 19, 1775, when a column of nearly 900 British Redcoats marched westward from Boston to arrest colonial leaders at Lexington and to seize war supplies at Concord. Ahead of the British column, Paul Revere rode across the countryside in the predawn darkness shouting, "The Regulars are coming out!" Revere's warning sparked a general alarm across Massachusetts that roused the minutemen to action.

Just after sunrise, the British column reached Lexington, where a militia company of seventy-seven men waited on the village green. Heavily outnumbered, the Americans had no thought of impeding the Redcoats but did want to make a display of Patriot resolve. Suddenly a shot rang out, and edgy British soldiers fired a volley at the Lexington company. A few Americans returned fire, but most scattered under the British onslaught. In a matter of seconds, seven militiamen were killed and nine wounded. (See figure 1-14.)

While the British column continued westward toward Concord, minuteman companies from across Massachusetts were marching hard toward Lexington and Concord. A thorough British search of Concord turned up few war supplies but gained the minutemen enough time to rally north of town. Around nine o'clock in the morning, a regiment of minutemen attacked three British infantry companies guarding the North Bridge over the Concord River. It was during this engagement that the "embattled farmers" fired "the shot heard round the world" that

1-14 British infantry fire upon Capt. John Parker's militia company on Lexington common just after sunrise on April 19, 1775. BROWN

1-16 The Minuteman Statue, sculpted by Daniel Chester French, stands near the North Bridge at Concord and marks the site where citizen-soldiers fired the "shot heard round the world." NPS

1-15 Amos Dolittle's detailed lithograph of the engagement at North Bridge. Heavy musketry from the minutemen (left) is prompting a British retreat (right). BROWN

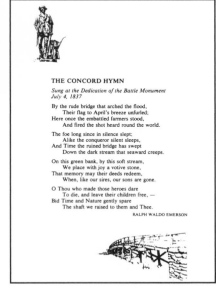

1-17 "The Concord Hymn" by Ralph Waldo Emerson immortalizes the actions of the minutemen at Concord Bridge. NPS

marked the beginning of the American Revolution and gave birth to the world's greatest democracy. (See figures 1-15 through 1-18.)

Around noon, the British column began a perilous, sixteen-mile retreat to Boston. Militia companies converged on the line of retreat and fired at the Redcoats from hidden positions behind trees, rocks, and stone fences. A 1,000-man British relief column that marched out to Lexington was the only thing that saved the original raiding party from all but certain annihilation. By sundown, the British had reached the safety of Boston, but not before nearly 4,000

1-18 According to tradition, the militiamen of Bedford, MA, carried this flag into battle on April 19, 1775. The flag is thought to be the oldest surviving banner in English-speaking America. **NARA**

militiamen had attacked them. On April 19, 1775, the Americans suffered 94 casualties and the British 272.

After Lexington and Concord, the Massachusetts militia laid siege to Boston. Heavy militia reinforcements appeared from Connecticut, Rhode Island, and New Hampshire. (See figures 1-19 and 1-20.) Meanwhile, a detachment of Vermont and Connecticut militiamen captured Fort Ticonderoga on the southern shores of Lake Champlain in the first American attack of the war. (See figure 1-21.)

On June 17, 1775, the militia army around Boston decided to occupy the Charlestown Peninsula on the north side of Boston harbor to put pressure on the Redcoats. The militia dug a sturdy redoubt on Breed's Hill, occupied a supporting line of stone and rail fences, and prepared additional defenses on Bunker Hill. (See figure 1-22.) Seeing an opportunity to crush an exposed portion of the militia army, the British ferried an assault force of over 2,000 troops to the Charlestown Peninsula. In a series of heroic but bloody assaults, the Redcoats managed to dislodge the Americans. (See figure 1-23.) However, the militiamen fought well and took pride in the fact that they severely bloodied one of the best

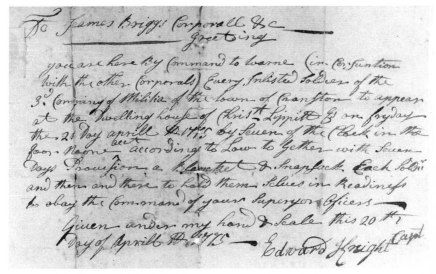

1-19 Militia Mobilization Order—issued in Cranston, RI, on April 20, 1775. It reads:

*To James Briggs Corporall Etc.*
*Greeting*
*You are here by command to warne (in conjunction with the other Corporals) every inlisted soldier of the 3d Company of Militia of the town of Cranston to appear at the dwelling house of Christ. Lipputt Esq on Fryday the 21 Day Aprill AD 1775 by seven of the clock in the foor noone acct according to law to gether with seven days provisions a blanket and knapsack each soldier and theirs and these to hold them selves in readiness to obey the command of your superior officers.*
*Given under my hand and seale this 20th day of Aprill AD 1775*
*Edward Knight Capt.*                                                    **NGEF**

1-20 A gunner of the Rhode Island Train of Artillery that acted as the first siege artillery during the investiture of Boston, 1775. **BROWN**

professional armies in the world. The battle of Bunker Hill cost the Redcoats 1,034 casualties, while the militia lost half as many. In time, the battle of Bunker Hill became an immortal symbol of the fighting spirit of the American citizen-soldier.

Realizing the need for a more permanent, standing army to fight a broadening war, the Continental Congress created the Continental Army on June 14, 1775, and appointed George Washington as its commander in chief. By early June, Washington was in Boston and working hard to establish "a respectable army." (See figure 1-24.) Congress eventually required the colonies to raise, organize, and equip regiments for the Continental

1-21 Connecticut Col. Benedict Arnold (with sword) and Vermont's Col. Ethan Allen jointly captured Fort Ticonderoga in May 1775. BROWN

1-22 Brig. Gen. Israel Putnam (CT), who had fought in the French and Indian War, was one of the commanders of militia forces surrounding Boston. BROWN

1-23 Militia men fight British grenadiers in this detail of the "Battle of Bunker Hill," a lithograph by Johnson Fry. BROWN

1-24 A member of the 1st Virginia Regiment in 1775. With military coats in short supply, many American units adopted colored hunting shirts, which were less expensive and yet gave a uniform appearance. NARA

1-25 An officer of Philadelphia's First City Troop, 1775. This unit's lineage predates the Revolution, and it continues to serve in the Pennsylvania Guard as Troop A, 104th Cavalry. **BROWN**

1-26 The Revolutionary War flag of the Philadelphia First City Troop, which is still displayed in their armory. **NARA**

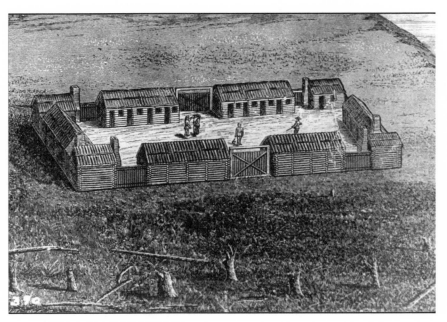

1-27 Boonesborough Fort was built and garrisoned by Kentucky militia in 1776 to protect settlers from Indian raids. **NARA**

Army that became known collectively as the "Continental Line." Throughout the war, each colony maintained an interest in sustaining their Continental regiments as well as their enrolled militia. The arrangement ensured that combinations of Continentals and militiamen would fight together in nearly all of the war's major engagements. (See figures 1-25 and 1-26.)

Throughout the American Revolution, the militia provided a vast reservoir of manpower for varying military needs while fighting in nearly all of the war's battles. The militia provided valuable reinforcements to the Continental Army and gave Washington the numbers of troops required to mount successful ripostes against the British. More than anything else, the militia prevented American Loyalists from gaining an upper hand. Militia patrols harassed British outposts, attacked Redcoat foraging parties, and monitored enemy troop movements. Other

1-28 Maj. Gen. Benedict Arnold in a French lithograph published in 1777. BROWN

1-29 The 1st Delaware Regiment stands its ground against British Regulars at the Battle of Long Island on August 27, 1776. The regiment went on to establish one of the finest combat records in the war. NGB

THE BATTLE OF TRENTON.

1-30 Washington's surprise attack on the Hessians at Trenton, NJ, capturing almost 900 prisoners, breathed new life into the dispirited Continental Army. BROWN

militia activities included suppressing Native American uprisings, repelling British maritime raids, enforcing local laws, garrisoning forts, guarding prisoners of war, transporting supplies, and patrolling against slave insurrections. (See figure 1-27.)

The militia made several significant contributions during the war's northern campaigns. In late 1775 Benedict Arnold's desperate but unsuccessful bid to capture Quebec was undertaken with a largely militia force. (See figure 1-28.) After the Redcoats abandoned Boston in March 1776, Washington moved the Continental Army to New York to thwart British efforts to capture the mouth of the Hudson River. Throughout ensuing battles in New York and New Jersey, the militia augmented the Continental Army. (See figures 1-29 and 1-30.) The militia's greatest achievement in the North came during the Saratoga

1-31 "There, my lads, are the Hessians!" Gen. John Stark shouted at the beginning of the Battle of Bennington, VT. "Tonight our flag floats over yonder hill, or Molly Stark is a widow!" Bennington was one of the few times militiamen in the Revolution defeated professional European soldiers in battle. BROWN

1-32 British Maj. Gen. John Burgoyne surrenders to Maj. Gen. Horatio Gates and Col. Daniel Morgan (in white hunting shirt) at Saratoga, NY, October 17, 1777. BROWN

1-33 The successful defense of Fort Moultrie on Sullivan's Island on June 28, 1776, during Britain's first attempt to capture Charleston, SC. BROWN

FORT MOULTRIE ON SULLIVANS ISLAND NEAR CHARLESTON, JUNE 28, 1776.

1-34 Lieut. Charles Cotesworth Pinckney was in the 1st South Carolina before the war and fought with it at Charleston in 1776. By 1777 he was commanding the regiment and later was a signatory on the U.S. Constitution. NARA

1-35 Col. Francis Marion, the "Swamp Fox," and his band crossing the Pee Dee River in South Carolina. NGEF

1-36 Maj. Gen. Nathanael Greene started the war as a private in the Rhode Island militia. BROWN

campaign of 1777. A British invading column from Canada faced increasing resistance from Continentals and militiamen as it moved south into the lower Hudson valley. On August 16, 1777, a small militia army defeated a significant portion of the invading army at the battle of Bennington and set the stage for a broader calamity. (See figure 1-31.) On October 17, the British finally surrendered at Saratoga, a dramatic development that convinced France to enter the war on the side of the Americans and to provide badly needed money, supplies, and troops. (See figure 1-32.)

In the southern campaigns, a dearth of Continentals resulted in the militia carrying much of the burden of the fighting. Early in the war, the militia had repelled British efforts to capture Charleston, South Carolina. (See figures 1-33 and 1-34.) After the debacle at Saratoga, the British decided to carry the war to the southern colonies. The royal occupation spawned a bloody guerrilla war that pitted British Regulars and Loyalist militia against a dedicated contingent of South Carolina militiamen. Operating from secure bases in thick woodlands and gloomy swamps, gifted leaders such as Thomas Sumter, Andrew Pickens, and Francis Marion mounted raids against Redcoat and Loyalist outposts. (See figure 1-35.) While Maj. Gen. Nathanael Greene led a wing of the Continental Army in the central Carolinas, militiamen scored important victories. (See figure 1-36.) At King's Mountain and Cowpens in late 1780 and early 1781, the Patriot militia defeated the Loyalist militia and humiliated British Regulars. (See figure 1-37.)

Eventually, the British Army evacuated the Carolinas and transferred its main effort to Virginia. At Yorktown, a combined force of

French troops and American Continentals, augmented by the French Navy and Virginia militiamen, encircled the British and forced their surrender on October 20, 1781. (See figures 1-38 and 1-39.) The debacle stopped further British military operations in America, and the American Revolution ended with the Peace of Paris on September 3, 1783.

Within weeks of the war's end, Congress moved to disband the

1-38 In 1780 a French officer drew this sketch of a member of the 1st Rhode Island Infantry plus a soldier from an unknown unit. The 1st RI was an all-black regiment assigned to the Continental Army. **BROWN**

1-37 Romantized lithograph of the American victory at Cowpens in 1781. **NARA**

1-39 John Trumbull's 1797 painting "Surrender of Cornwallis at Yorktown." **LC**

**1-40 Discharged American soldiers of the Continental Army march in their last parade in New York, 1783. BROWN**

Continental Army. (See figure 1-40.) On June 2, 1784, national military forces reached an historic nadir: only eighty broken-down veterans remained to guard military stores at West Point, New York, and Fort Pitt in western Pennsylvania. Yet, the needs for a strong military were clear. Great Britain still remained a potential threat, and Native Americans strongly opposed white settlement beyond the Appalachians. In 1786 a popular uprising in Massachusetts, known as Shay's Rebellion, convinced most Americans of the need for a centralized government with adequate military power.

The Founding Fathers met in Philadelphia in 1787 to draft the U.S. Constitution. One of the most vexing debates of the Constitutional Convention was centered on the composition and missions of U.S. military forces. One side argued stringently for a strong Regular Army; the other ardently supported a continued reliance on the enrolled militia.

**1-41 The U.S. Constitution made the militia a permanent part of America's military establishment. NARA**

**1-42 President Washington reviewing the troops at Harrisburg, PA, during the Whiskey Rebellion, October 3, 1794. NGB**

In the end, the Constitution mandated a dual American military system composed of the Regular Army and the militia. (See figure 1-41.) The Constitution granted Congress the power to call out the militia for three specific purposes. Article I, Section 8, reads: "To provide for calling forth the Militia to execute the Laws of the Union, suppress Insurrections and repel Invasions."

In 1791 the passage of the Second Amendment guaranteed "the right of the people to keep and bear arms" as the best way of maintaining "a well regulated Militia" against the possible abuses of a strong federal government gone awry. The following year, Congress enacted the Militia Act of 1792, which prescribed the administration of the militia and authorized an Adjutant General (AG) to head the militia in each state. For more than a century, the act governed the administration of citizen-soldiers and identified the militia as primarily a state rather than a federal institution.

The militia's first major test following the Revolution came in 1794 when a popular uprising in western Pennsylvania against liquor taxes challenged the authority of the federal government. With Regular troops fully engaged elsewhere, President George Washington called out the militia to put down the Whiskey Rebellion. (See figure 1-42.) Four states provided nearly 13,000 men to march on the insurgents, and the overwhelming show of force quickly restored order. The Whiskey Rebellion established the militia as a reliable, national instrument for maintaining domestic order.

# TWO

# The Volunteer Militia, 1795–1902

## The Jefferson Era

In the twenty years following the Whiskey Rebellion, the states took some actions to place the militia on a more permanent footing. A common practice was to partition a state into militia "divisions" that were geographic recruiting districts rather than tactical organizations. In addition to the state AG, governors appointed militia generals to oversee recruiting and training in each district. The local company remained the backbone of the militia system. As in colonial times, towns in the North and counties in the South remained the basis of company organizations. States began to purchase weapons and to issue them from arsenals. (See figure 2-1.)

The election of Thomas Jefferson in 1800 as the third president brought a strong supporter of the militia to the head of the government. Jefferson identified the militia as one of the "essential principles of our government." The key tenets of Jefferson's military policy were "the supremacy of the civil over the military authority" and "a well-disciplined militia—our best reliance in peace and for the first months of war, till Regulars

2-1  Detail of an 1809 enlistment certificate, New York State Artillery, showing the men wearing black bicorn caps. NGEF

may relieve them." Jefferson forged defense plans that relied on a strong Navy, coastal defenses, the militia, and a small Regular Army. In the event of an enemy invasion, local militia forces were to contain the hostile forces until Regulars arrived. Together, Regulars and militiamen would push the enemy back into the sea. (See figure 2-2.)

Jefferson's espousal of the militia as one of the country's defensive pillars prompted an appraisal of its preparedness. Not until 1804 was the War Department able to determine that 525,000 men were enrolled and organized into a hodgepodge of

regiments and brigades. Proper weapons were not available to arm units adequately. While militiamen often performed ably as a local force to protect property or to enforce laws, it became clear that state soldiers were far from ready to perform as a coherent, national defense force. In 1808 Congress authorized an annual allotment of $200,000 for the purchase and distribution of weapons on the basis of annual state strength reports. At the going rate of $13 dollars per musket, the appropriation purchased approximately 15,000 new weapons each year.

2-2 Detail of 1812 enlistment certificate, New York State Militia, showing artillerymen in bicorns and light dragoons in "Tarleton" helmets. BROWN

## The War of 1812

In the decades following the Revolution, many Americans believed that England sought to humiliate and limit the growth of the United States. On the high seas, English warships regularly stopped U.S. vessels and impressed Yankee seamen into the British Navy. At the same time, British forts in lower Canada posed a direct threat. When Anglo-American relations deteriorated further, Congress reluctantly declared war on Great Britain on June 18, 1812.

With a Regular Army that numbered only 6,686 officers and men, military leaders concluded that professional soldiers acting by themselves were too small to mount major attacks against Canada and that offensives could only take place with substantial participation from the militia. The War of 1812 revealed glaring inadequacies in the militia system and raised serious questions regarding the responsibilities the federal government and the states shared for the common defense. The New England states opposed the war and failed to support military operations. The governors of Connecticut and Massachusetts initially refused to send their militiamen off to war. The defiance of the New England states denied the country some of its best organized militia units and greatly affected American strategy. Unable to mount an offensive from New England against Montreal or Quebec, the United States resorted to attacks against British forces around the Great Lakes.

Operations along the Canadian border revealed additional weaknesses in the militia system. Relations between Regular Army and militia generals suffered from petty jealousies and an unwillingness to cooperate. Both refused to relinquish control of their troops for the sake of fostering better unity of effort and simplicity of command. When an American force surrendered to the British near Detroit in August 1812, the Regular Army blamed the war's first fiasco on the militia's ineptness, ill-discipline, and insubordination. On as many as half a dozen occasions, Ohio and New York militia units refused to cross into Canada to attack British positions. The New York militia's reputation suffered two black eyes in the summer of 1813 when citizen-soldiers failed to turn out in sufficient numbers to prevent British raiding parties from looting Plattsburgh and Buffalo. The incidents embarrassed militia advocates who had long argued that these soldiers would fight to the death to defend home and hearth. (See figure 2-3.)

However, under competent and aggressive leadership, militiamen performed creditably. William Henry Harrison, who had led a militia army to victory over the Native Americans at the battle of Tippecanoe in central Indiana in 1811, again arose as an effective militia leader. In September 1813 Harrison led a large, mixed force of 3,500 Regulars and militiamen into Ontario and smashed the British and their Native American allies on October 5 at the battle of the Thames River. (See figure 2-4.)

On August 19, 1814, an invading column of 4,000 Redcoats landed on the western shore of Chesapeake Bay and marched on Washington, D.C. A general alarm across Maryland, Virginia, and the District of Columbia resulted in the concentration of an odd assortment of 5,000 militiamen and Regulars near Bladensburg, Maryland. In the ensuing battle on August 24, a number of Army Regulars, Marines, and militiamen stood their ground until overrun, but a majority of the ill-trained militia units retreated with such ease that the action became known as the "Bladensburg Races." The

2-3 Fort Meigs, located near Toledo, OH, was defended by a brigade of Virginia and Pennsylvania militia during the winter of 1812–13. BROWN

2-4 "Colonel Johnson's Mounted Men Charging a Party of British and Indians at Moravian Town, October 2, 1813." Also known as the "Battle of the Thames" in Ontario, Canada, the Kentucky militia cavalry broke the enemy line and totally routed the British Army. BROWN

British entered Washington and torched the Capitol, the White House, and a number of other public buildings.

The Redcoats experienced an altogether different reception at

Baltimore two weeks later. Under determined leadership and with more time to prepare, Regulars and militiamen presented an effective defense. When British infantry landed north of Baltimore, militiamen blocked their advance from a formidable line of field fortifications. At the battle of North Point on September 13, the Maryland militia turned back the invaders and inflicted considerable casualties. Meanwhile, a garrison of Regulars and militia stubbornly and successfully defended Fort McHenry against a punishing British naval bombardment that went on for twenty-four hours and inspired Francis Scott Key to jot down verses that eventually became the "Star-Spangled Banner."

The militia's most dramatic display of bravery came at New Orleans under the command of Andrew Jackson. A combat veteran at the age of thirteen, "Old Hickory" established a well-deserved reputation as the resourceful and iron-willed leader of the Tennessee militia. In a daring bid to capture New Orleans and possibly sever Louisiana from U.S. control, the

British landed 5,300 soldiers just below New Orleans. To defend the Crescent City, Jackson cobbled together a diverse fighting force of 4,700 soldiers that included two regiments of Regulars; militiamen from Tennessee, Kentucky, and Louisiana; aristocratic gentry and free blacks from New Orleans; a band of Choctaw Indians; and pirates under Jean Lafitte. (See figure 2-5.)

After a series of preliminary skirmishes against the Americans, the Redcoats decided to carry out a direct frontal assault against Jackson's main defenses. Attacking in an early morning fog on January 8, 1815, the British made little headway against Jackson's strong earthworks. Sheltered behind bales of cotton, the Americans achieved a concentration of firepower that mowed down the orderly British ranks. In the end, the Redcoats suffered 2,400 casualties, while Jackson

lost about seventy soldiers. Word soon arrived in Louisiana that the War of 1812 had ended on December 24, 1814, with the Treaty of Ghent, a full two weeks before the battle of New Orleans. In the popular mind, Jackson's lopsided victory reinforced the notion that American militiamen, hastily assembled and with scant training, could easily triumph over a better-prepared enemy.

## The Rise of the Volunteer Militia

Following the War of 1812, the enrolled militia entered a period of neglect and decline. The second victory over Great Britain and the continued elimination of serious Native American threats against western expansion caused most Americans to question the value of mandatory military service. The militia's uneven record in the war convinced a larger segment of society that the protection of the nation might rightly belong to professional soldiers. Over time, the enrolled militia system simply became unmanageable. Increases in the nation's population resulted in a massive, theoretical militia enrollment that neither the federal government nor the states could adequately resource or administer. Throughout the enrolled militia's ranks, shopkeepers and factory workers supplanted yeoman farmers, and urban laborers viewed musters as a waste of time and energy and the purchase of arms and equipment as an unnecessary burden. In many

2-5 Maj. Gen. Andrew Jackson at the battle of New Orleans, January 1815. NGEF

2-6 An 1820s lampoon of a militia muster. BROWN

states, muster days started with the roll call and quickly degenerated into a daylong indulgence of heavy drinking, wild gambling, and crude profanity. (See figure 2-6.) Ironically, the notion of universal, obligated service that was at the very heart of the enrolled militia concept finally produced a situation of near-universal unreadiness.

The creeping rot that afflicted the enrolled militia after the War of 1812 accelerated with each passing decade. In 1831 Delaware completely abolished mandatory service. Massachusetts eliminated compulsory service in 1840, while Indiana that same year classified its men by age and required only the youngest to attend musters and training. Maine, Ohio, and Vermont eliminated the enrolled militia in

1844; Connecticut and New York in 1846; Missouri in 1847; and New Hampshire in 1851. By the middle of the 1840s, the enrolled militia system had all but faded away into obsolescence.

However, an expanded network of volunteer militia companies emerged to infuse the concept of the citizen-soldier with renewed vigor. Volunteer companies drew together those with an affinity for the military lifestyle and the pomp and circumstance of the parade route and the drill field. The units all shared a number of common traits. New members required some form of sponsorship, and bylaws governed membership requirements, the election of officers, unit organization, the wearing of uniforms, the types of

weaponry and equipment required, and the frequency of social and military activities. Members normally paid dues and bore all of the expenses of uniforms, weapons, and accoutrements. While the enrolled militia system included men wherever they dwelled, the volunteer militia was concentrated mostly in urban centers. Because volunteer companies were a source of camaraderie and hosted scheduled activities, unit musters occurred at least monthly or as often as one night per week. The frequency of unit meetings produced the tradition of volunteer citizen-soldiers attending regular drill periods. Increased unit activity resulted in a demand for adequate facilities, and volunteer companies sought public buildings suitable for

2-7 An 1820s watercolor of a militia dragoon. BROWN

2-9 Other commands sported uniforms patterned on styles popular with European armies, such as the Polish-influenced "chapska" helmets worn by the "Boston Lancers" in the 1830s. BROWN

2-8 Many volunteer units in the 1820s–30s adopted uniforms based on then-current U.S. Army dress, such as this officer of the "Washington Grays" (PA) wearing a Model 1822 shako. BROWN

meetings, social activities, and the storage of weapons and equipment.

Volunteer militia companies often formed themselves into specialized units of infantry, cavalry, and artillery. As the elite troops of the armies of the day, grenadiers and light infantrymen formed the flank companies of regiments deployed in battle and assumed the position of honor at ceremonies and parades. Volunteer infantry companies organized as grenadiers and light infantry jealously protected their position of honor at public ceremonies. The states welcomed cavalry and artillery units because maintaining such organizations in the enrolled militia was difficult and expensive. The states often

provided funds to defray the greater costs of purchasing and maintaining horses, cannons, saddles, and ammunition. (See figures 2-7 through 2-10.)

A volunteer militia unit was the first military organization in the United States to adopt the title "National Guard." The use of the name came about as the result of a visit to New York by the Marquis de Lafayette, the famous French hero of the American Revolution. Volunteer militiamen from the 2d Battalion, 11th Regiment of Artillery, comprised the honor guard for Lafayette. In observance of his visit on July 14, 1825, the battalion voted to rename itself the "Battalion of National Guards" in tribute to Lafayette's command of the Parisian militia, the Garde Nationale. (See figure 2-11.) (The battalion later became the famous 7th New York Regiment in 1847 and serves in the New York Army National Guard today as the 107th Support Group.)

Perhaps the most widely recognized characteristic of volunteer militia companies was martial ardor that found its expression in extravagant uniforms and dramatic unit names. With the Regular Army wearing dark blue, state soldiers often wore some shade of gray, and company names often hinted at the color and style of the uniform volunteers sported. Ethnicity often determined the type of dress, and companies of Irishmen in green jackets, Highlanders in kilts, Germans in hunting hats, and Frenchmen in full, red trousers tramped down America's streets. Elite infantry units adopted uniforms and head-gear—towering bearskin hats were a favorite—that accentuated their height and physical presence. Titles of most units were descriptive, such as Rifles, Guards, and Cadets, while names like Invincibles, Avengers, and Terribles

**2-11 The Marquis de Lafayette is greeted by the New York State Militia on July 14, 1825. NGB**

2-10  Some volunteer companies mixed uniform patterns combining both U.S. and European styles. Among them were the "Newark City Guard" (NJ) wearing 1822 shakos and English-styled coats. BROWN

2-12 Young's Yaegers" was composed entirely of German immigrants in 1830s Baltimore, MD. Yaegers were elite German riflemen. BROWN

were intended to instill unit pride.

Volunteer militia companies also formed along occupational and ethnic lines. Skilled workers often banded together to emphasize their status in society. Volunteer companies proliferated among immigrants, especially the Germans and the Irish. (See figure 2-12.) The meeting halls and armories of immigrant companies allowed an environment that re-created their European roots. Gathered together in their militia company, immigrants could speak their native tongue without embarrassment, drink the spirits of the home country, and enjoy a congenial, familiar atmosphere. Immigrants considered membership in an American volunteer company as the soundest possible display of patriotism toward their adopted country. New York City and New Orleans hosted an abundance of ethnic militia companies. As a backlash, native-born Americans formed their own exclusive units whose names and uniforms stressed the history and culture of the United States.

Volunteer companies fostered a sense of community through frequent social and philanthropic activities. Among the more popular events were gala balls where citizen-soldiers, resplendent in their distinctive uniforms, feasted and danced the night away with wives and sweethearts. (See figure 2-13.) Theatrical performances and concerts were popular social events and effective fundraisers. In addition, companies raised money for orphans and destitute families. Volunteer companies were prominent at public ceremonies and celebrations.

Despite the emphasis on social and ceremonial events, militiamen recognized that volunteer companies were primarily military organizations. The most common manifestation of military training was weekly drill periods in which citizen-soldiers practiced the intricate tactical maneuvers of the day. Parades and drill competitions provided an opportunity for companies to compare their relative strength and proficiency. Marksmanship training was a popular training event, especially when held as a competition between units. Encampments that included groupings of volunteer companies were important training events in many states. The typical encampment lasted a few days and included extensive drill periods

2-13 A handbill announcing a "Grand Military Ball" being held by Delaware's "Dover Artillery" as a fund-raising event in January 1846. BROWN

and long road marches. (See figures 2-14 and 2-15.)

## The Mexican War

By the 1840s, many Americans believed that the United States should extend all the way from the Atlantic to the Pacific Ocean. However, Mexico included most of the western lands not acquired under the Louisiana Purchase and blocked America's westward expansion. A long simmering dispute between the United States and Mexico finally precipitated a major war. Soldiers of the Republic of Texas had gained independence from Mexico with bloody fighting at the Alamo and the battle of San Jacinto in the spring of 1836. Nearly a decade later, the United States offered statehood to Texas. Mexico, however, had never fully recognized Texan independence and broke diplomatic relations with the United States. By May 1846 a state of war existed between the two powers.

For the first time, the United States waged a war on foreign soil. The demise of the enrolled militia system and memories of citizen-soldiers refusing to cross the border and of a few states

2-14 Often volunteer companies would visit "brother" units in other states for a round of mock battles, parades, and feasting. In July 1844 the "Boston City Greys" were hosted by several Baltimore, MD, units for four days. BROWN

2-15 Detail of "Camp Thompson—Encampment of the Springfield Light Guard at Double Beach, Branford, Connecticut—August 25, 1846." Local encampments allowed the men to practice military skills such as the posting of perimeter guards around their camp. BROWN

2-16 Jefferson Davis, c. 1860. MHI

2-17 American forces, including the "Mississippi Rifles," storm the "Bishop's Palace" in Monterrey, Mexico, on September 22, 1846. BROWN

unwilling to support the War of 1812 prompted a major change in defense policy. While combinations of Regulars and militiamen had fought all previous wars, the nation relied for the most part on volunteer regiments. In simplest terms, volunteer regiments were citizen-soldier units raised by the states for federal service and did not exist in peacetime. However, militia traditions and laws hung heavily over the raising of volunteer units. The states assumed the responsibility for mobilizing volunteer regiments, volunteers elected their own company officers, and the governors appointed more senior officers up to the rank of colonel. Altogether, the United States mobilized just short of 116,000 Regulars, volunteers, and militiamen. Of the total manpower effort, 75 percent were citizen-soldiers who served

2-18 "The Gallant Charge of the Kentuckians at the Battle of Buena Vista, February 23, 1847, and the complete defeat of the Mexicans." BROWN

alongside Regular Army units.

Despite the preponderance of volunteer units, the militia made significant contributions. At the outbreak of war, Texas and Louisiana provided 12,601 militiamen for immediate service, and many of these subsequently joined volunteer and Regular

Army units as individuals. In many cases the states first turned to volunteer militia companies to form their federal volunteer regiments.

Perhaps the best example of a volunteer regiment raised from state troops was the Mississippi Rifles. Commanded by Col.

Jefferson Davis, the Mississippi Rifles established a combat record comparable to that of the best Regular Army regiments. (See figure 2-16.) A West Point graduate, Davis served several years in the Regular Army before resigning his officer's commission in 1835. Ten years later, he was elected to the U.S. House of Representatives but resigned his seat to command troops in the Mexican War. Returning to Mississippi, he led the men of the Mississippi Rifles with distinction at the battles of Monterrey and Buena Vista. Davis's insistence on good order and discipline and the arming of his soldiers with the best rifled weapons available made his unit one of the premier regiments of the Mexican War. At the battle of Buena Vista, where 90 percent of the American Army consisted of volunteer units, an unwavering performance by the Mississippi Rifles and two Indiana regiments, together with the superior fire of Regular Army artillery, broke the main Mexican attack.

A number of militia-based regiments performed with distinction during the war's most crucial battles and campaigns. In northern Mexico, militia-based volunteer regiments gained fame at the battles of Monterrey and Buena Vista. (See figures 2-17, 2-18, and 2-19.) Volunteer militia regiments comprised the bulk of the troops that formed Maj. Gen. Winfield Scott's invasion force against central Mexico. (See figure 2-20.) In the campaign for the capture of Mexico City, citizen-soldier

2-19 "Death of Lieut. Col. Henry Clay, Jr., of the Second Regiment of Kentucky Volunteers at the Battle of Buena Vista, February 23, 1847." The 2d Kentucky Infantry played a critical role in blunting a Mexican attack threatening the center of the American position. Henry Clay Jr. was the son of former secretary of state and speaker of the house of representatives, Henry Clay. BROWN

2-20 "Landing of the American Forces under General Scott at Vera Cruz (Mexico), March 9th, 1847." Among the troops with Scott were volunteer regiments from LA, KY, TN, PA, SC, and IL. BROWN

regiments fought well at Cerro Gordo and in other battles. (See figures 2-21 and 2-22.)

The victory in the Mexican War sparked renewed interest across the country in military affairs, and volunteer militia companies prospered. (See figure 2-23.) Volunteer militia companies flourished while emphasizing

2-21 "The Battle of Cerro Gordo, Fought April 17th 1847." This American victory, which routed the Mexican Army, opened the road through the mountains to Mexico City. BROWN

2-22 The wooden leg of Mexican President Santa Anna was captured by members of Company G, 4th Illinois Volunteer Infantry, at the end of the Battle of Cerro Gordo. Santa Anna lost his leg in an earlier war, so he was forced to wear this replacement. He fled from Cerro Gordo on horseback so fast he left it, and $18,000 in gold, in his personal carriage. ILNG

2-23 Detail of the "Honorable Discharge" certificate of Pvt. William Herbert, a member of the "Reading Artillery," Reading, PA, August 1st, 1848. It clearly portrays the less-ornate uniform adopted by many volunteer units during the 1840s. BROWN

2-24 "Encampment of the Washington Light Infantry of Charleston, S.C., at Orangeburg." c. 1850. BROWN

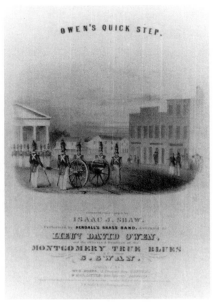

2-25 Sheet music cover "Owen's Quick Step" of the "Montgomery True Blues," an artillery battery from Montgomery, AL, c. 1850. During the antebellum period, many volunteer units had their own bands that played distinctive unit "marches" to build esprit de corps. NGEF

2-26 *Harper's Weekly* ran this lithograph of the "Rover Guards" of Cincinnati, OH, during the company's visit to New York City in 1859. The men are dressed in red coats and blue trousers and are wearing the 1855 shako. BROWN

their social and military value. (See figures 2-24 through 2-27.) At the same time, a looming sectional crisis over states' rights and slavery heightened a sense of awareness regarding military preparedness.

The militia's greatest advo-

2-27 One of the units sponsoring the visit of the Rover Guards was the 7th Regiment, New York State Militia, commanded by Col. Abraham Duryea in 1859. Note the "NG" for "National Guard" on the gorget around his neck. BROWN

cate in the 1850s was Elmer Ellsworth. (See figure 2-28.) While a struggling law student in Chicago, Ellsworth eked out a living as a militia drillmaster. It was at this time that he met a Frenchman who had served with a Zouave regiment in the Crimea, and the soldier of fortune taught Ellsworth the intricate, peculiar commands and motions of Zouave drill routines. In 1859 Ellsworth was elected to the command of a volunteer militia company that he reorganized as the United States Zouave Cadets of Chicago. Ellsworth's men learned the rapid, gymnastics-like movements of the Zouave drills and adopted a picturesque costume complete with red cap, sash, and baggy trousers. The Zouave Cadets filled Chicago's streets with crowds eager to watch their rapid, intricate drills.

Ellsworth's fortunes changed dramatically when he gained employment as a legal clerk in Abraham Lincoln's law firm in Springfield, Illinois. Lincoln and Ellsworth became friends and discussed possible militia reforms for Illinois. In the summer of

2-28 Col. Elmer E. Ellsworth in 1861. BROWN

2-29 Members of the "Richmond Grays," Company A, 1st Regiment, Virginia Volunteers on duty for the execution of John Brown in Charles Town, VA, (now WV) in November 1859. The company, organized in 1844, is perpetuated today by the 276th Engineer Battalion. VANG

1860, Ellsworth, now a colonel in the Illinois militia, gained national notoriety when the Zouave Cadets undertook a tour of twenty cities. Across the Midwest and the Northeast, the Zouaves dazzled crowds with drilling, marching, firing, and wild bayonet exercises. Dozens of Zouave militia companies formed in the wake of the national tour. At the end of the excursion, Ellsworth returned to Illinois as the most renowned militiaman in the nation. When Abraham Lincoln left for Washington to assume the presidency in early 1861, Ellsworth accompanied him as a bodyguard.

## The American Civil War

A raid by the rabid abolitionist John Brown on the federal arsenal at Harpers Ferry, Virginia, in October 1859 was the first of a violent chain of events that finally caused the outbreak of the American Civil War. For nearly thirty years, the North and the South had drifted farther apart politically and socially on the issues of states' rights and slavery. Although many abolitionists were pacifists, some staunch abolitionists in the North, such as Brown, believed that moral suasion and political action had failed to stem the spread of slavery and that violence was the only remaining remedy. Many Southerners began to think that secession was preferable to remaining in the Union.

News of John Brown's unsuccessful but bloody raid on Harpers Ferry hardened opposing views above and below the Mason-Dixon Line. Many Southerners believed that northern radicals had intended all along to use force to limit the rights of the states, destroy slavery, and threaten the southern way of life. After Harpers Ferry, both sides anticipated war, and new militia companies sprang up all over the country that focused on preparedness rather than pageantry. (See figures 2-29, 2-30, and 2-31.) The election of Republican Abraham Lincoln in November 1860 on a platform that severely restricted the expansion of slavery made Southerners livid and deepened the nation's political divide.

South Carolina responded to Lincoln's election by seceding from the Union, and by February

## Abraham Lincoln: The Militia President

Abraham Lincoln was born into poverty in a log cabin in Hodgenville, Kentucky, in 1809. He moved with his family to Indiana in 1816 and finally to Illinois in 1830. Two years later, the governor of Illinois called out the militia in a campaign against the Indians. The chieftain Black Hawk led the Sacs in a series of actions to reclaim territories they had given up by treaty. Young Abraham Lincoln joined a militia company and was elected captain. When it appeared that his unit would not see service, many of its members disbanded and went home. However, Lincoln volunteered as a private in a militia scout unit, sometimes called the "Independent Spy Battalion." Lincoln said later that no success gave him as much personal satisfaction as his time in the Illinois militia.

After the Black Hawk War, Lincoln successfully pursued law and politics and maintained an interest in militia affairs. He served with the Illinois legislature in 1834–41 and in the U.S. House of Representatives during 1847–49. In 1860 Lincoln was elected the sixteenth president of the United States and became perhaps the most outstanding president in American history. Guided by great wisdom, sound judgment, and extraordinary common sense, Lincoln led the country through its darkest hours and was successful in preserving the Union and freeing the slaves. As commander in chief, Lincoln proved an adept strategist who realized that destroying the armies of the Confederacy was more important than capturing Richmond or seizing other strategic points.

1861 six other southern states had left the Union and banded together to create the Confederate States of America. On April 12, 1861, Confederate troops fired on Fort Sumter in Charleston harbor. (See figure 2-33.) After the fort's surrender, four additional states joined the Confederacy, and the Confederate government, headed by President Jefferson Davis, established its capital in Richmond.

As America split in two, volunteer militia companies across the South were the primary agents of state governments in seizing control of federal forts, arsenals, customs houses, and mints. (See figure 2-34.) In Charleston, militiamen seized a federal arsenal and occupied fortifications that Union troops abandoned when they evacuated to Fort Sumter. Georgia volunteer companies took Fort Pulaski at the mouth of the Savannah River, and Alabama soldiers occupied two Union forts that controlled the entrance to Mobile Bay. In Florida and Louisiana, militia units captured the arsenals at Apalachicola and Baton Rouge, respectively. Virginia militiamen

2-30 Corp. Issac Pierce (left) and Sgt. Charles Griffin, both members of the 1st Battery, Massachusetts Light Artillery, in 1861. MHI

2-32 President Abraham Lincoln, c. 1860. MHI

2-31 Pvt. William Brittain, Company C, 9th Battalion, Georgia State Guard Cavalry, in a prewar uniform, c. 1860. He is holding an M-1842 pistol and light cavalry saber. MHI

2-33 Officers of the "Washington Light Infantry" of Charleston, SC, in camp on Sullivan's Island near Charleston, 1861. MHI

took control of the Norfolk Navy Yard, and in Arkansas, four militia companies forced federal troops to abandon Fort Smith without a fight. The blatant attack on Fort Sumter galvanized the North.

On April 15, President Lincoln ordered 75,000 militiamen into federal service for ninety days to put down the insurrection. The War Department apportioned troop quotas to the states, established mobilization sites, and set May 20 as the muster day for all units. The North's top priority was to secure its capital, and the first troops to provide for Washington's defense were thirty-eight militia companies from the District of Columbia. Five companies from Pennsylvania were the first state troops to reach Washington. Massachusetts was the first state to forward a complete regiment to the capital. (See figures 2-35 and 2-36.)

Throughout the spring of 1861, most northern states rushed regiments in various

2-34 Members of the "Perote Guards" Company H, 5th Louisiana Volunteer Infantry, stand beside two ten-inch Columbiads of the "Perote Sand Batteries" at Fort Barrances, Pensacola, FL, in 1861. MHI

2-35 "Attack on the 6th Massachusetts Volunteer Infantry at Baltimore on April 19th, 1861." MHI

degrees of preparedness to Washington. Several regiments adopted the Zouave uniforms and drill methods that Elmer Ellsworth had promoted before the war. (See figures 2-37 and 2-38.) By early summer, thirty-five regiments, consisting of 37,000 soldiers, were encamped near the nation's capital. (See figure 2-39.) In northern Virginia, the Confederacy managed to concen-

trate an army of its own: thirty-two regiments, numbering 33,000 troops. (See figure 2-40.) Volunteer militia companies formed the basis for a significant number of the regiments on both sides.

In a twist of fate, Elmer Ellsworth became the North's first national hero. His national

**2-36 Men from Company A (Trenton), Mercer Brigade, New Jersey State Militia, who answered the call for ninety-day volunteers to protect Washington, DC, were later awarded the "First Service Medal" by a grateful state. NGEF**

**2-38 One of the most famous photographs of the Civil War is this young member of the 4th Michigan Volunteer Infantry, c. 1861. MHI**

**2-37 An officer and men of the 4th Michigan Volunteer Infantry, who adopted the uniform of the French "Zouaves," including white gaiters and fez caps, c 1861. MHI**

reputation permitted him to recruit quickly the 11th New York Volunteers, a Zouave regiment. On May 24, 1861, the 11th New York crossed into Virgina to occupy Alexandria. Colonel Ellsworth noticed a Confederate flag waving defiantly from the roof of a hotel in the heart of town. Accompanied by a detachment, the regimental commander hurried to the hotel, climbed to the roof, and cut the flag down. However, a shotgun blast from the hotel's proprietor killed Ellsworth instantly. As the first Northern regimental commander killed in the Civil War, Ellsworth's death created a national sensation. A bereaved Abraham Lincoln hosted the funeral at the White House, and songs and poems across the nation celebrated Ellsworth's exploits.

2-39 Volunteers of the 7th New York Infantry "National Guard" at Camp Cameron, Washington, DC, in 1861. Note the "NG" sign on the tent. MHI

On July 21, 1861, northern troops attacked the Southern army at the battle of First Bull Run. By any standard, the war's first major battle was a confused,

2-40 An unknown South Carolina battery, c. 1861. MHI

2-41 Looking more like Union soldiers, these members of an unknown company of the 1st Georgia Volunteer Infantry are wearing blue frock coats and caps, c. 1861. MHI

2-42 Militiamen of the "Clinch Rifles," Company A, 5th Georgia Infantry, in 1861. The first pattern or "National" Confederate flag is suspended from the tent pole. (The photographic process made the "CR" on the tent and bucket appear backward.) MHI

amateur affair. The ranks of antebellum militiamen and raw volunteers displayed poor discipline, and officers demonstrated their inexperience in handling formations under fire. The convention of Union blue and Confederate gray uniforms did not yet exist, and the tendency of militia units to wear blue or gray without regard to regional affiliation resulted in friendly fire incidents. (See figure 2-41.) What could have been an orderly retreat for the North turned into a rout as inexperienced soldiers panicked. Equally unseasoned Southern troops were too exhausted and confused to exploit their victory.

The defeat at First Bull Run shocked the North and prompted even greater efforts. Realizing that the small Regular Army and regiments based on volunteer militia companies were inadequate for a broader war, President Lincoln on July 25, 1861, called up 500,000 volunteers for up to three years of service. Many of the militia-based regiments in the North that had responded to the first call-up after Fort Sumter immediately reformed as volunteer regiments. In the South, a similar pattern emerged as militia units and volunteers combined to create Confederate regiments. (See figures 2-42 and 2-43.) Many Southern states formed their own troops for local duty, but as the war progressed, the Confederate government took control of these troops as well. The exact number of Civil War

2-43 Soldiers of Company L, 1st Texas Infantry, part of "Hood's Brigade" in the Army of Northern Virginia, standing in front of their log hut used as winter quarters while stationed at Dumfries, VA, in 1861–62. MHI

2-44 In May 1863 these gunners of the 1st Connecticut Battery posed before the battle of Chancellorsville, VA. MHI

2-45 Officers and men of the 3d Indiana Cavalry, part of the Army of the Potomac, November 1864. MHI

2-46 A gun section of the Washington Artillery of New Orleans, part of the Army of Northern Virginia, fires from its position on Marye's Heights at advancing Union soldiers during the climax of the battle of Fredericksburg, VA, on December 13, 1862. LC

regiments formed from antebellum militia units is almost impossible to determine, but usually the lower-numbered regiments in each state contained significant numbers of militiamen. (See figures 2-44 and 2-45.) On both sides, militia-based regiments accrued outstanding combat records. In the North, the 1st Minnesota Volunteer Infantry gained glory second to none for its heroic charge at Gettysburg, and the Washington Artillery of New Orleans became one of the South's most outstanding fighting units. (See figure 2-46.)

Antebellum militia units provided a wealth of military experience to the armies and often served as a training base. Prewar militiamen were prepared to drill and maneuver troops and often rose to high command and staff positions. New York's 7th Regiment provided 600 officers to the Union Army. The Artillery Corps and the First Troop, City Cavalry of Philadelphia, together provided nearly 250 officers. A number of militia officers on both sides rose to senior command. (See figures 2-47 through 2-51.)

The state militia systems provided significant service throughout the war. Northern states furnished militia units that served independently or in conjunction with federal troops to hold forts, protect coastlines and the Canadian border, garrison the Indian frontier, and guard Confederate prisoners.

In performing these functions, the militia relieved federal troops for duty elsewhere. Militiamen also monitored subversive political activities, tracked down deserters, and helped put down violent draft demonstrations. To ensure enough manpower for the war, Massachusetts once again instituted the

enrolled militia in 1864 for men between the ages of eighteen and twenty-four. Rhode Island, West Virginia, Ohio, and Indiana as well instituted forms of compulsory militia service at various times. In 1861 Connecticut became the first state to adopt the title "National Guard" for its militia units, and the

2-47 Maj. Gen. Benjamin F. Cheatham commanded Tennessee volunteers in the Mexican War. He was appointed a major general of Tennessee militia before serving as one of the most respected division commanders in the Confederate Army. NARA

2-48 Maj. Gen. Lew Wallace served as a lieutenant in the 1st Indiana in the Mexican War. He was commanding an Indianapolis militia company when the Civil War started in 1861. His excellent combat record brought him quickly up the ranks. After the war, he served as the AG of Indiana. Despite a distinguished war record, Wallace is best remembered as the author of the novel *Ben Hur*. NARA

2-49 Lt. Gen. Thomas J. Jackson from Virginia, graduated from West Point in 1846 and saw combat as a Regular in the Mexican War. In the 1850s he became a professor at the Virginia Military Institute (part of the Virginia militia establishment) with the state rank of major. At the battle of First Manassas, he gained fame as "Stonewall" for the stubborn defense by his brigade, forever to be known as the "Stonewall Brigade." Its lineage is carried today by the 116th Infantry, 29th Infantry Division (Light). MHI

following year the Empire State officially changed the designation of its militia forces to "The National Guard of the State of New York." Pennsylvania and Ohio raised state regiments for limited, local service that bore the title "National Guard" in their designations. In the South, militiamen manned coastal defenses, guarded Northern prisoners, and maintained aggressive patrols that tracked down runaway slaves and deserters. As Union troops advanced further into the South, militiamen increasingly fought alongside the volunteer regiments of the Confederate Army.

The states produced large numbers of militiamen on short notice in response to unexpected emergencies. When the Confederate Army invaded Kentucky in the fall of 1862, Ohio's governor declared a militia levee, and 15,000 citizen-soldiers rallied to defend Cincinnati. Further east, the Pennsylvania militia served on active duty for two weeks during the Antietam campaign. The summer of 1863 was a particularly busy time for Northern militia units. In response to Lee's second invasion of the North, militiamen from Pennsylvania, New York, and Rhode Island augmented the Army of the Potomac during the Gettysburg campaign. Ohio and Indiana militiamen turned out in large numbers to repel a raid north of the Ohio River by southern marauders under John Hunt Morgan. By the end of the Civil War, militiamen on both sides had participated in nearly every aspect of America's bloodiest war. (See figure 2-52.)

## The Rise of the National Guard

The volunteer militia's lowest ebb occurred between 1865 and 1877. At first, the militia in the northern states all but ceased to exist. Exhausted by the Civil War, men were not interested in voluntary military service. No threat seemed imminent, and the Regular Army appeared entirely capable of handling Indian affairs in the West and the occupation of the South without assistance from the militia. By one count, less than one-third of all the states maintained any semblance of a militia.

2-50 Maj. Gen. Ambrose E. Burnside served as a major general in the Rhode Island militia prior to 1861. Despite a checkered war record, he later served three terms as Rhode Island's governor. **NARA**

2-51 Maj. Gen. Daniel Butterfield served as the first sergeant of the "Clay Guards" of the District of Columbia militia before the war. He rose to the position of chief of staff of the Army of the Potomac, but is perhaps best known as the composer of the bugle call "Taps." **NARA**

2-53 Illinois militiamen fire on a mob during the railroad strike of 1877. LC

2-52 Many of the postwar Guard leaders got their start during the conflict. Among them was 1st Lt. Frank Welch, one of the few black officers serving during the war. In the war he was a member of the famed 54th Massachusetts Volunteer Infantry (Colored); in the 1880s he organized and commanded an African American battalion in the Connecticut Guard. MHI

militia. However, ten years after the Civil War, militia organizations began to appear. Perhaps nostalgic for the excitement and camaraderie of field duty, veterans banded together in volunteer units. By 1875, volunteer militia strength stood at 90,865 nationwide.

The Great Railroad Strike of 1877 thrust the militia back onto the national scene. When strikers snarled rail traffic from St. Louis to Boston that summer, fifteen states called out approximately 45,000 militiamen. The militia's performance varied widely. In some cases, militiamen fired on strikers, while in other instances they united with the workers. (See figure 2-53.) Federal troops, police forces, and militiamen finally brought the situation under control but not before 100 people were killed and hundreds more injured. The strike served as a watershed event in the transformation of the state militias into the National Guard. In response to the violence, a number of states increased militia budgets and raised additional units.

The poor performance of some state units resulted in the introduction in Congress of proposals for militia reform legislation. The soldiers were in a poor position to produce a reform bill of their own. While a number of states had their own militia associations at the time, no such national organization

2-54 Maj. Gen. Dabney H. Maury of Virginia was a West Point graduate who proved a talented commander of Confederate forces during the war. In the postwar period he founded the Southern Historical Society in 1868 and helped to create the National Guard Association of the United States in 1878. MHI

existed. Under the guiding leadership of an ex-Confederate, Maj. Gen. Dabney H. Maury, concerned militia leaders met for the first time in Richmond in 1878 to discuss militia reforms and the creation of a national lobbying group. (See figure 2-54.) The following year, the National Guard Association of the United States (NGAUS), the nation's oldest and most successful military lobbying organization, came into existence. (See figure 2-55.) NGAUS scored its first major victory in 1887, when Congress doubled the militia's annual allotment to $400,000.

As settlers pushed westward beyond the Mississippi River to carve new states and territories from the wilderness, they formed militia groups. Citizen-soldiers provided protection against bandits and vigilantes, guarded prisoners, acted as posses, controlled riots in the cities, safeguarded officials and helped to settle disputes over ranch, water, and mining claims. A principle function of local militias was to provide security against Indian attacks and to launch reprisal raids. On the Pacific coast, California created the most substantial militia forces in the West. Kansas developed the most respectable militia organization on the Plains. In the Southwest, New Mexico created the most credible force of citizen-soldiers. (See figures 2-56 and 2-57.)

However, postbellum militia organizations differed significantly from citizen-soldier units

2-55 As the Guard sought to increase its professionalism after the Civil War and railroad riots, a monthly publication expressly to share information among the states was created in 1877. NGEF

2-56 Members of Wyoming's "Cheyenne Guard" march in a parade in the 1880s. NGB

before the Civil War. While Guard units still thrived as social organizations, they placed more emphasis on military readiness. The experience of the Civil War convinced these soldiers to make regiments the basis of their postbellum organizations rather than separate companies. Most states adopted the Regular Army's plain field uniform for normal duty and retained their extravagant uniforms for solemn ceremonies and formal portraits. (See figures 2-58 through 2-64.) By 1879 many states had formally adopted the

2-57 A Nevada officer of the "Virginia City Blues" in 1886. NGEF

2-58 Officers and men of Company A, "Bowling Green Guard," 3d Battalion, Kentucky State Guard, at the Yorktown Centennial celebration, October 1881. BROWN

2-59 A private of the 1st Infantry, Vermont Militia, Yorktown Centennial celebration, October 1881. BROWN

2-60 Capt. George N. Walker of the "Chatham Artillery" of Savannah, GA, Yorktown Centennial celebration, October 1881. BROWN

title "National Guard." Across the nation Guard units moved into new armory buildings large enough to support a regiment's administrative, training, and recreational activities. Armories were to have a distinct, military look, and architects employed towers, turrets, and parapets of heavy stone to make armories an imposing sight. (See figures 2-65 and 2-66.)

By 1895 the National Guard was well established across the country. Personnel numbers stood

New Hampshire's "Yorktown Battalion," October 1881. BROWN

2-62 In May 1887, to celebrate the centennial of the U.S. Constitution, all the states were invited to send Guard units to participate in a four-day "National Encampment" consisting of drill competitions and parades on the mall in Washington, D.C. Eighteen states sent at least one unit. Among them was Company A, "Volunteer Southrons," 1st Mississippi Infantry. LISTMAN

2-63 Company D, 1st Minnesota Infantry, won the "Second Prize" in the drill competition at the National Encampment in Washington, D.C., in May 1887. LISTMAN

2-64 Philadelphia also held a celebration to mark the 100th anniversary of the Constitution in September 1887. One of the units attending the festivities was the Washington Cadet Corps, District of Columbia National Guard. Among this group of officers is Capt. Christian Fleetwood (back row, right with two medals), who was awarded the Medal of Honor during the Civil War. LISTMAN

2-65 Dedication of the 7th New York Infantry's armory in October 1880. NGEF

2-66 The "Chickasaw Guards and their Armory, Memphis, Tennessee, 1881" as published by *Harper's Weekly,* July 2, 1881. BROWN

2-67 Members of Company C, "Tacoma Guard," 1st Infantry, National Guard of Washington, in full marching order leave for annual training at Camp Black Diamond, WA, July 1891. WSHS

2-68 Company H, 1st Regiment, South Dakota National Guard, on mobilization day for the Spanish-American War, April 30, 1898. NGEF

at 115,699 strong, making the Guard more than four times larger than the Regular Army. All forty-three states and three of the four territories, Alaska excepted, maintained Guard units. In terms of capabilities, the Guard included approximately 94,000 infantrymen, 5,500 artillerymen, and 7,000 cavalrymen. (See figures 2-67, 2-68, and 2-69.)

## The Spanish-American War and the Philippine Insurrection

The explosion and sinking of the USS *Maine* in Havana harbor in Cuba on the morning of February 15, 1898, ignited a long-simmering conflict between Spain and the United States over Cuban independence. Americans blamed the explosion on Spanish sabotage, and war cries were heard across the country. Congress declared war against Spain on April 22 with the goal of securing Cuban independence. By war's end, America was set upon the world stage as an imperial power with colonies in the Caribbean, the central Pacific, and East Asia.

At the time, the Regular Army numbered only 28,000 men, far too few to invade the major Spanish colonies in the Caribbean—Cuba and Puerto Rico—and to occupy the Philippines. President William McKinley called on the states to raise 125,000 men for overseas service. Once again, the federal government looked to the governors to raise volunteer regiments. However, the presidential call-up stipulated that

2-69 Some Guard units entering active duty for the war against Spain were better prepared than those in the early days of the Civil War. One area in which the Guard had tried to improve its performance was marksmanship. A number of states held shooting competitions with the award of medals to the high scorers, such as this 1890s example from New York. NGEF

2-70 Four officers of the 1st Maryland Volunteer Infantry stand in the snow around their tents at Camp MacKenzie, GA, December 1898. NARA

2-71 Training camps were often crowded and unsanitary, such as this one at Anniston, AL. NARA

all men filling the first volunteer units had to come from existing militia organizations. With the popularity of the war, entire regiments of enthusiastic militiamen mustered into the Army for two years, and 194 militia units served during the period.

The volunteer regiments soon boarded trains for hastily constructed training camps either in the South or on the West Coast. Health concerns were not seriously considered, and troops arrived to find poor drinking water and unsanitary conditions. These factors led to the biggest killer of the war: disease. Far more American soldiers died from malaria, yellow fever, typhoid, and typhus than from bullets. Militiamen spent almost all of their time drilling, marching, and learning the proper handling and care of their arms and equipment that was often old and worn out. (See figures 2-70, 2-71, and 2-72.)

By June many of the regiments in the southern camps were ready to go to Cuba. War

2-72 Members of the 3d Alabama Volunteer Infantry, one of nine African American units serving on active duty during the war. Only one saw brief combat and two others were deployed to Cuba as garrison in Havana. NARA

plans called for the capture of Santiago, the base of the Spanish fleet, and the capital at Havana. Most of the units identified for the invasion were Regular Army, however two state units, the 2d Massachusetts and the 71st New York, sailed for Cuba with the Regulars. (See figure 2-73.) Perhaps the most famous American unit of the war, the 1st U.S. Volunteer Cavalry, popularly known as the "Rough Riders," included one New Mexico National Guard cavalry squadron and two troops from the Arizona Guard. Theodore Roosevelt, a former New York Guardsman, was instrumental in raising the regiment and served as its lieutenant colonel. (See figure 2-74.)

By June 24 most of the men had landed in Cuba while advance parties probed toward Santiago. The Spanish took up good defensive positions along a series of heights protecting Santiago, including Kettle and San

2-73 Men of the 71st New York Volunteer Infantry marching in Cuba in 1898. This watercolor is one of a number painted by Pvt. Charles Johnson Post, a member of the unit during the war. CMH

Juan Hills. Teddy Roosevelt and the Rough Riders first charged up Kettle Hill and then against San Juan Hill, gaining fame for themselves. Among the first to reach the top of Kettle Hill were Guardsmen from two New Mexico cavalry troops. The cost was high; twenty Rough Riders died as did fifteen members of the 71st New York Infantry, the only other militia unit in the assault. After the capture of the heights, U.S. artillery bombarded Santiago harbor and the city surrendered on July 17. With the signing of a

2-74 Lt. Col. Theodore "Teddy" Roosevelt posing with members of the "Rough Riders" on San Juan Hill, Cuba, July 1, 1898. Some of these men were prewar members of the Arizona National Guard. LC

2-76 This rifle pit in Ponce, Puerto Rico, was captured by members of the 3d Wisconsin Volunteer Infantry, July 29, 1898. NARA

2-75 Soldiers of the 2d Wisconsin Volunteer Infantry advance through the streets of Ponce, Puerto Rico, July 29, 1898. LC

general armistice on August 12, a number of militia regiments deployed to Havana to garrison the capital. They returned home after the peace treaty granting Cuban independence was ratified in March 1899.

As the fighting ended in Cuba, American troops invaded Puerto Rico. The clear majority of the invading force was Guard units. During the last week of July, U.S. troops landed on the southern shores of the island. (See figures 2-75 and 2-76.) According to plan, these groups moved cross-country toward the capital of San Juan to besiege it from the land side while the Navy blockaded from the sea. The advance encountered only minimal resistance, and the Americans quickly occupied San Juan. The Army immediately established permanent garrisons, with all of the militia units returning home by the end of 1898.

With the campaigns in Cuba and Puerto Rico completed, only one theater of war remained. The Philippines in the Southwest Pacific was of particular strategic value to the United States as a naval base in East Asia. Before the war, the Filipinos had an independence movement directed against the Spanish authorities. Gen. Emilo Aguinaldo commanded 15,000 guerrilla fighters on the main island of Luzon who waged a hit-and-run war against the

2-77 Troops of the 1st Nebraska Volunteer Infantry wade a river during the Philippine Insurrection, Luzon, Philippines, April 1899. NENG

Spanish.

On June 30, the first American troops landed near Manila and joined Aguinaldo's guerrillas. En route, the 2d Oregon Infantry had landed with U.S. Marines on the island of Guam to claim it as an American territory. There was great tension between the Americans and the guerrillas, but they decided to act together. Additional militia reinforcements increased the U.S. presence to 11,000 men, enough to take the city without participation from Aguinaldo's forces. After secret talks with the Spanish, the governor agreed to surrender Manila to the Americans. On August 13, Manila fell

2-78 A skirmish line of the 2d Oregon Volunteer Infantry during the Philippine Insurrection, 1899. Three members of this regiment were among the twenty Guardsmen awarded the Medal of Honor in the Philippines. NARA

into American hands with only sporadic resistance. Unknown to anyone in the Philippines, the belligerents had signed an armistice ending the war the day before the attack.

Over the next months, an uneasy alliance developed between U.S. authorities and Aguinaldo as the Spanish withdrew and a new American colonial government was established. Additional militia regiments arrived to strengthen the U.S. garrison. After months of tension, Aguinaldo's forces finally launched coordinated attacks on several American outposts on the night of February 5, 1899, and the Philippine Insurrection was under way. Militiamen repelled these attacks with few casualties and then went on the attack. Over the next few weeks, the Americans and Filipinos took turns launching hit-and-run raids against each other, resulting in increased losses on both sides. (See figure 2-77.)

On March 25, the Americans went on the offensive to capture the rebel capital at Malolos, sixty miles north of Manila. After a grueling six-day advance, they captured the smoldering ruins of Malolos; the rebels had fallen back to their new capital at San Isidro. In mid-April the Americans advanced toward San Isidro. During this march, twenty soldiers made National Guard history by earning the Medal of Honor. A group of volunteers from the 1st North Dakota and 2d Oregon Infantry (see figure 2-78) became the vanguard of the column, leading the advance under the command of a local American civilian, William Young. Known as "Young's Scouts," they first stormed across a burning bridge under intense enemy fire, saving it for the American advance. Later they were surrounded and cut off in a small village. During several hours of desperate fighting, the scouts repelled numerous enemy assaults, and every man was wounded at least once. All thirteen survivors were awarded the Medal of Honor, and seven additional state soldiers earned the Medal of Honor during the

2-79 Pvt. Frank L. Anders, Company B, 1st North Dakota Volunteer Infantry Regiment of Militia, in December 1894. During the Philippine Insurrection, he earned the Medal of Honor as a member of "Young's Scouts." MHI

2-80 The quick and successful end of the Spanish-American War led many states to award their own medals to honor the men returning home. This "War With Spain Medal" was issued by Missouri. NGEF

campaign. (See figure 2-79.)

At home, operations in the Philippines generated sharp debates. Many Americans did not favor involvement in the Philippines, and they demanded that citizen-soldiers come home. The men had enlisted to fight for Cuban independence, not to subdue the Philippines.

By August 1899 all militia units had arrived back in their states. (See figure 2-80.) In all, the militia had made the occupation of Puerto Rico and the capture of the Philippines possible, adding greatly to American gains during the war. The credible performance of state soldiers in the Spanish-American War suggested that the National Guard was about to enter a new epoch.

# THREE

# The National Guard, 1903–1945

## The Birth of the National Guard

At the beginning of the twentieth century, the United States was flush with success from victory in the Spanish-American War. In control of overseas possessions that stretched from the Caribbean to the Philippines, America sought parity with the European powers and began an expansion of its armed forces. A more modern Navy came into existence, and various plans circulated for the expansion of the small Regular Army that numbered only 66,000 soldiers. Advocates of land power argued for a larger standing Army that could guard America's new possessions and compete with European armies.

In 1900 the National Guard consisted of 116,542 officers and enlisted men. New York was the largest Guard state, with 13,869 soldiers; Nevada was the smallest, with two companies of infantry. All Guardsmen served voluntarily without compensation, and in many cases, soldiers paid unit dues and provided their own uniforms. Responding to calls for increases in the size of the Regular Army, Guard advocates argued that a large

3-1 Maj. Gen. Charles Dick, 1903. NGEF

standing Army was inconsistent with traditional American political beliefs. Guardsmen believed that a properly trained, equipped, and manned National Guard could provide the country with an organized reserve to augment the Regular Army during national emergencies.

The Militia Act of 1903 temporarily settled the issue by transforming all state militia units into the organized regiments and companies of the National Guard. In simplest terms, Guard units received

increased funding and equipment, and in return, they were to conform to federal standards for training and organization. The law recognized two classes of militia; the National Guard under federal-state control and the Unorganized Militia, the mass of eighteen- to forty-five-year-old males available for conscription. The act required Guardsmen to attend twenty-four drill periods and five days of summer camp per year and continued the practice of Guard soldiers attending drill periods on one work night each week. For the first time, Guardsmen received pay for summer camp. The law called for Guard units to conduct maneuvers with the active Army and to receive training assistance from Regulars. The Guard became subject to federal call-ups for nine months, though its service was restricted to within U.S. borders.

## The National Guard, 1903–1916

The Militia Act of 1903 had a widespread and immediate impact on the National Guard. Soldiers gladly accepted federal aid while assuming responsibility for improvements in training and

3-2 Guardsmen from nine states took part in the Manassas Maneuvers in Virginia in 1904. **NARA**

organization. The first federally funded maneuvers by Guardsmen and Regulars occurred in 1904. (See figure 3-2.) The War Department issued nearly 90,000 magazine rifles to Guardsmen, and new field pieces went to National Guard artillery batteries. By 1911 National Guard organizations had reorganized themselves into standard units of Infantry, Field Artillery, Coast Artillery, Cavalry, Engineers, and Signal. (See figures 3-3 and 3-4.) The flood of new weapons and equipment and the need for property accountability and maintenance resulted in calls for more adequate armories. No federal monies were allotted for armories, so states, counties, and towns

## Senator Charles W. F. Dick: Father of the Modern National Guard

Charles William Frederick Dick enjoyed a long life of public service dedicated to the National Guard and the nation. He was born in November 1858, in Akron, Ohio, where he attended public schools and studied law. In 1894 Dick opened his own law practice and became active in politics.

Charles Dick's military career began in 1885, when he volunteered in Company B, Eighth Regiment, Ohio Infantry. One year later, he became the company commander. Over the next fourteen years, Dick rose to the rank of lieutenant colonel, and in 1898 he served with the Eighth Ohio in Cuba.

After the Spanish-American War, Dick was elected to the U.S. House of Representatives in November 1898. In March 1904 he was elected to the U.S. Senate and served there until losing a reelection bid in 1911. During his years as a member of Congress Dick championed the Militia Act of 1903 and its 1908 amendments. During Dick's service in Congress, his military career flourished. In 1900 he became the commander of the Ohio Division, National Guard, with the rank of major general. In 1902 he was elected president of the National Guard Association of the United States (NGAUS), and he held that position for seven years.

After leaving the Senate in 1911, Dick resumed his law practice. He ran for the U.S. Senate in 1922 but lost the election. Charles Dick lived long enough to see his labors bear great fruit during the massive National Guard mobilizations for World Wars I and II. He died in Akron, Ohio, on March 13, 1945, at age eighty-six and is buried in Glendale Cemetery.

had to pool their financial resources. A rash of armory expansions and new construction took place across the country. (See figure 3-5.) Heartened by its new status, the Guard's strength grew to 132,194 soldiers by the end of 1916. (See figures 3-6 and 3-7.)

Before long, the modern National Guard assumed its first major mission in defending the American homeland from foreign attack. The new overseas possessions acquired during the Spanish-American War placed a greater burden on the Army's limited

3-4  California Guardsmen armed with Krag-Jorgensen magazine rifles patrol the streets of San Francisco in the wake of the devastating earthquake of 1906. NARA

3-3  Company H, Arkansas National Guard, at mess during annual training at Camp Riley, KS, in August 1906. MHI

3-5 Among the new facilities being built for Guard use was this mess hall at Camp Perry, OH, site of the National Guard Rifle Matches. NGEF

3-6  With the number of Guardsmen increasing after 1903, a magazine to address their concerns started publication in 1907. Unlike the earlier *National Guardsman* printed in the 1870s, this periodical had numerous illustrations of units training, such as these Colorado men on the pistol range. NGEF

coastal defense resources. In 1907 the Army admitted that it needed additional forces to man the increased number of coastal defenses overseas and at home. Congress soon passed legislation authorizing the National Guard to serve in the Coast Artillery. Regular Army Coast Artillery units were to man all overseas defenses and half of the fortifications in the United States, while Guardsmen assumed responsibility for the remaining defenses. In all, fifteen states organized Coast Artillery companies. By 1912 the Guard had created 126 Coast Artillery companies with a total strength of 8,186 soldiers that manned fortifications along the East, West, and Gulf coasts. (See figures 3-8 and 3-9.)

Important amendments to the Militia Act of 1903 came in 1908. Time and geographic limits for Guard service disappeared, and the law specified that Guardsmen would go to war as units and not as individual replacements. A Division of Militia Affairs was established within the War Department. The staff division was filled with Regular officers who had overall responsibility for the administration of the Guard. By 1911 the Division of Militia Affairs came under the direct control of the Army chief of staff, and Congress elevated the division head position to general officer rank.

Another important development occurred in 1915 with the activation of the Guard's first

3-7 Guard officers had to train like their Regular counterparts, in this case map reading in 1912. VANG

3-8 Members of the District of Columbia Coast Artillery Battalion load a shell during annual training at Fort Monroe, VA, 1910. NGEF

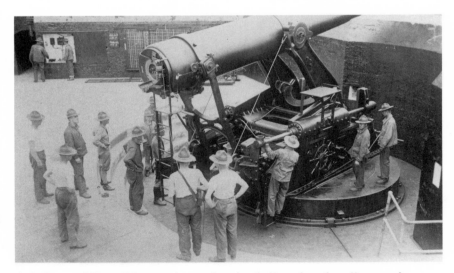

3-9 One of Fort Monroe's twelve-inch "peek-a-boo" guns is ready to be fired by men of the District of Columbia's Coast Artillery Battalion, 1910. NGEF

flying unit. New York's 1st Signal Company had experimented with balloons since 1908, and it was natural for the Empire State to take the lead in heavier-than-air flight. The first Guard aviator went aloft in 1911, when Beckwith Havens of New York took to the skies in an early Curtis aircraft. On May 22, 1912, Lt. Col. Charles B. Winder of Ohio became the first Guard officer to obtain a reserve military aviator rating. (See figure 3-10.) The New York National Guard activated the 1st Aero Company in 1915, and the

following year a second aviation company was formed in Buffalo. (See figure 3-11.) At the same time, Guard aviators in California, Ohio, and Michigan made some progress in organizing flying units and obtaining pilot ratings.

## The National Defense Act of 1916

In August 1914 Americans watched anxiously as Europe plunged into the throes of World War I. Within a year, the fighting had degenerated into a bloody stalemate. Anticipating involvement in the war, a preparedness movement swept across America that emphasized physical fitness and marksmanship. In Washington, the War Department advocated a "Continental Army" drawn from national reservists as the best means for building an army suitable for European warfare. A sharp debate ensued over the best means for providing a large army, and in the end arguments favoring the National Guard carried the day.

The National Defense Act of 1916 was an important watershed in National Guard history. The act specifically designated the National Guard as the Army's primary reserve while authorizing an expanded Regular Army and Army Reserve. Henceforth, all state units would be designated as National Guard. The president received authority to mobilize the National Guard for the entire duration of national emergencies. The number of annual drill periods increased from twenty-four to forty-eight, with pay provided for all drills. Summer camp was extended from five to fifteen days. Guard units received formal federal recognition after achieving specified manning and equipping levels.

## The Mexican Border Call-Up

Only fifteen days after passage of the National Defense Act of 1916, the National Guard responded to its first twentieth-century call to active federal service. Tensions between the United States and

3-10 Ohio's Lt. Col. Charles Winder in 1912. NGEF

3-11 Men of the 1st Aero Company, New York National Guard, in formation with their aircraft, 1916. NARA

3-12 Advertising for recruits in Cambridge, MA, during the Mexican border mobilization, 1916. MAMM

3-13 Cavalrymen of Rhode Island's 1st Squadron load their horses on the train that will move them to Brownsville, TX, 1916. NGEF

3-14 Infantrymen of a Massachusetts regiment march out of camp near El Paso, TX, during their deployment along the Mexican border in 1916. MAMM

Mexico had increased in previous years. In early 1916 a civil war raged in Mexico. Hoping to solidify his position as a dominant Mexican warlord, Francisco "Pancho" Villa conducted a cross-border raid against Columbus, New Mexico, on the night of March 9, 1916, killing seventeen Americans. In response, President Woodrow Wilson ordered a large punitive expedition of Regulars into northern Mexico to track down the bandits, and the president asked the governors of Texas, New Mexico, and Arizona to provide Guardsmen for border protection. By May 11, 5,260 Guardsmen were headed for the border.

The Army's punitive raid, consisting of 10,000 Regulars under the command of Brig. Gen. John J. "Black Jack" Pershing,

made slow progress. On June 16, the Mexican government warned Pershing to advance no further. Fearing a growing crisis with Mexico, President Wilson ordered a partial call-up of the National Guard on June 18. (See figure 3-12.) In all, 158,664 Guard soldiers reported for duty, including New

York's 1st Aero Company, the first Guard flying unit to be called to active duty, although it did not deploy to the border. Critical shortages in equipment and transportation initially impeded the mobilization, but problems abated over time. (See figure 3-13.) Within six weeks, 112,000 Guardsmen

3-15 Guardsmen patrol a sand dune in southern Arizona looking for cross-border raiders from Mexico, 1916. NGEF

3-17 1st Lt. (and future thirty-third president of the United States) Harry S. Truman was a member of the 1st Separate Battalion, Missouri Field Artillery (note "Mo." on collar), in 1917. During World War I, he commanded Battery D, 129th Field Artillery, 35th "Santa Fe" Division. NARA

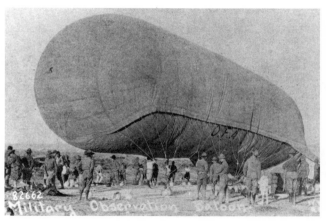

3-16 Artillerymen of Ohio's 1st Field Artillery prepare an observation balloon for ascent while stationed in Texas during the border crisis. NARA

from across the nation were along the Mexican border. Though they saw no combat, the mobilization proved valuable. (See figures 3-14 and 3-15.) The states became familiar with the complexities of moving great numbers of troops, and commanders received experience in handling large troop formations. (See figure 3-16.) Individual Guardsmen benefited from better training and physical conditioning. By the early spring of 1917, the crisis had passed, and

most Guardsmen headed home only to face an even greater emergency.

## The National Guard in World War I

By early 1917 tensions between the United States and Germany had erupted into open hostilities. On April 6, 1917, America declared war on Germany. In Europe, the exhausted Allied armies on the Western Front welcomed the news of large reinforcements from America. (See figure 3-17.)

Much of America's initial combat power came from the National Guard. In April 1917, 66,594 Guardsmen were still serving along the Mexican border. Over a period of weeks, Guard units came on active duty and recruiting efforts intensified. (See figures 3-18 and 3-19.) By August 5, the entire National Guard—379,701 troops in all—was on active duty at mobilization camps across the nation, training and organizing for combat. The Army determined that a new tactical formation was required for the demands of trench warfare and directed the creation of "square" infantry divisions. Guardsmen busied themselves organizing square divisions that contained two

3-18 A Washington state National Guard recruiting station, with its static display of small arms and .30 caliber machine gun, encouraging men to join the Guard in the early days of World War I. WSHS

3-19 World War I recruiting poster. NGEF

3-20 Members of Battery F, 111th Field Artillery (VA), 29th Division, move their three-inch gun into position while training at Camp McClellan, AL, 1917. VANG

3-21 Tent inspection of Michigan's 128th Ambulance Company, 32d Division, Camp MacArthur, TX, 1917. NGEF

3-22 Two riflemen of the 40th "Sunshine" Division take aim on the "enemy" during field exercises at Camp Kearny, CA, May 1918. NARA

3-23 A gas bomb explodes while members of the 40th Division practice trench tactics, Camp Kearny, CA, May 1918. NARA

brigades and a total of four infantry regiments. Eventually, the Guard formed sixteen divisions numbered 26 through 41. (See figures 3-20 through 3-26.)

A rush developed to get American combat troops to France. The Army's 1st Division and the National Guard's 26th "Yankee" Division, composed of troops from New England, arrived in France almost simultaneously. (See figure 3-27.) The third division to arrive was the Guard's famous 42d "Rainbow" Division. The 42d was the seventeenth Guard division formed for World War I and earned the name "Rainbow" because its units were drawn from twenty-six states and the District of Columbia, a geographic dispersion that arched across the country like a rainbow. Despite the eagerness to get American troops into the fray,

3-24 Members of the 31st "Dixie" Division leave the "Gas House" at Camp Wheeler, GA, February 1918. NARA

3-25 While most of the Army deployed overseas, four regiments of Texas Cavalry were raised from the Guard to maintain security along the Mexican border. NARA

3-26 The only campaign medal ever authorized expressly for Guardsmen by the Congress was the "Texas Cavalry Medal." It was awarded to the men who served in the four regiments of Texas Cavalry, who were ineligible for the Allied Victory Medal. NGEF

3-27 Members of the 101st Infantry (MA), 26th Division, await an order to attack while training in the snow before being committed to combat in France, January 1918. MAMM

3-28 Soldiers of the 107th Infantry (formerly 7th NY Infantry), 27th "Empire" Division, charge across "no man's land" during the Somme Offensive, November 1918. NARA

3-30 Men of Company K, 110th Infantry (PA), 28th Division, return from the front, Meuse, France, September 1918. NARA

3-29 Maj. Gen. John F. O'Ryan (right), commander of the 27th Division, watches as the division passes in review for 2d Army commander, Maj. Gen. George Reed, Somme, France, November 1918. NARA

3-32 Two members of Pennsylvania's Battery A, 108th Field Artillery, 28th Division, wear their gas masks while receiving a fire mission during the battle of St. Mihiel, September 1918. NARA

3-31 A driver of the 109th Ambulance Company, 28th Division, points to machine gun holes made by a strafing German airplane, August 1918. NARA

3-33 Men of the 30th "Old Hickory" Division search prisoners taken in the Aisne region of France, October 17, 1918. NARA

3-34 A machine gun section of Company B, 117th Infantry (NC), 30th Division, at Bibeauville, Aisne, France, October 19, 1918. NARA

3-35 Gunners of the 120th Field Artillery (WI), 32d "Red Arrow" Division, struggle with a 75mm field piece in the mud of France, 1918. MHI

General Pershing, now commander of the American Expeditionary Forces (AEF), insisted that his troops had to receive thorough training before entering the trenches. (See figure 3-28.)

However, a huge German offensive in March 1918 prompted the early commitment of American troops. The 26th and 42d Divisions went into battle, soon followed by the Pennsylvanians of the 28th "Keystone" Division. During weeks of severe fighting in the St. Mihiel Salient, in the Ramieres Wood, and along the Marne River, Guardsmen showed their fighting ability. In September General Pershing committed the AEF to the clearing of the St. Mihiel Salient. Afterward, the Americans successfully attacked the heavily defended German sector in the Argonne Forest. (See figures 3-29 through 3-43.)

3-36 Guardsmen of the 131st Infantry (IL), 33d "Prairie" Division, man a temporary trench and await a possible German counterattack, Forges, Meuse, France, October 3, 1918. NARA

**3-37** Members of the 108th Military Police Company, 33d Division, guard canal barges carrying supplies to the front along the Meuse River, October 26, 1918. **NARA**

**3-38** Battery C, 130th Field Artillery (KS), 35th "Santa Fe" Division, prepares to open fire in September 1918. **NARA**

**3-39** Using basic tools, men of Company D, 111th Engineer Regiment, 36th "Texas" Division, repair a road at Boureuilles, Meuse, France, September 26, 1918. **NARA**

**3-40** These soldiers of the 147th Infantry (OH), 37th "Buckeye" Division, were the first members of the division to capture German prisoners, Luneville, France, August 14, 1918. **NARA**

3-41 Capt. E. Popp, of the Chemical Company of the 38th "Cyclone" Division, questions a German prisoner, October 6, 1918. NARA

3-42 Sighting his weapon, a member of Company C, 150th Machine Gun Battalion (WI), 42d Division, trains prior to entering combat, France 1918. NARA

3-43 Taking a break from the front, men of the Headquarters and Machine Gun companies of the 166th Infantry (OH), 42d Division, "play ball," Summercourt, France, October 18, 1918. NARA

3-44 African American Guardsmen of the 369th Infantry (NY), 93d "Blue Helmet" Division, train in trenches near Maffrecourt, France, in May 1918. Assigned to French divisions, they were issued French helmets, rifles, and equipment, making resupply easier. NARA

Black Guardsmen distinguished themselves on the Western Front. The famous 369th Infantry—formerly the 15th New York—fought under French command, where it earned the nickname "Hell Fighters from Harlem," was awarded the French Croix de Guerre, and suffered more losses than any other American black regiment. (See figure 3-44.) Two other black Guard regiments distinguished themselves in battle. The 370th Infantry—formerly the 8th Illinois—and the 372d Infantry, composed of black Guard units from a number of states, made up the bulk of the troops assigned to the all-black 93rd Division, the eighteenth Guard division credited for service in World War I.

At the beginning of World War I, approximately 100 qualified Guard pilots were available for service. Though no National Guard aviation unit went to war, Guard flyers made important contributions. For example, Colonel Raynal C. Bolling, the original commander of New York's 1st Aero Company, helped to establish training centers in Europe for American fliers. (See

3-45 Col. Raynal C. Bolling. NARA

3-46 Kansan 2d Lt. Erwin B. Bleckley received a posthumous Medal of Honor. KSNG

3-47 Another Guardsman to earn the Medal of Honor was Corp. Jake Allex, Company H, 131st Infantry (IL), 33d Division. He single-handedly killed or captured more than twenty Germans in a machine gun position that had devastated his company. ILNG

figure 3-45.) Other Guard officers filled important aviation staff positions. Four Guardsmen became aces during aerial combat. Second Lt. Erwin B. Bleckley, a Kansas artilleryman who volunteered for duty as an aerial observer, became the first Guard aviator to receive (posthumously) the Medal of Honor, when German ground fire downed his aircraft during a desperate mission over the Argonne Forest. (See figure 3-46.)

By the end of the war in November 1918, the AEF had grown to 2.1 million Americans. Overall, 433,478 Guardsmen served in World War I. Of the forty-three American divisions sent to France, eighteen of them—about 40 percent of the entire AEF—were National Guard. Guard divisions suffered a total of 103,721 killed or wounded, approximately 43 percent of American casualties. Guardsmen from North Carolina, South Carolina, and Tennessee who made up the 30th Division received twelve Medals of Honor, more than any other division in the AEF. Perhaps the best tribute to Guardsmen came from their

3-48 After the armistice of November 1918, there were many ceremonies to attend, such as this one involving the 106th Field Signal Battalion (GA), 31st Division, at Bracieux Loir et Cher, France, December 1918. NARA

3-49 Though the fighting was over, Guardsmen continued to train, as demonstrated by these members of Florida's Battery B, 140th Field Artillery, 39th "Delta" Division. They are moving their 155mm field guns by use of a Cadillac tractor, Le Valdahon, France, February 1919. NARA

3-50 Corp. Milburn Ellsworth of Company C, 162d Infantry (OR), 41st "Sunset" Division, was a guard at the AEF Headquarters in Paris, France, in April 1919. Note that he's wearing his division's patch. While waiting to go home, the use of distinctive unit shoulder patches spread throughout the Army. NARA

enemies. The German High Command considered eight American divisions especially effective; six of those were National Guard. (See figures 3-47 through 3-52.)

## The National Defense Act of 1920

Unfortunately, Guardsmen returned home triumphant in 1919 only to face a serious challenge to their continued existence. Flushed with victory in World War I, planners on the Army's General Staff in the War Department pressed for a large standing army to support America's new interests as an international power. The Army drafted an ambitious plan calling for a standing force of 500,000 Regulars backed by a vast reservoir of 500,000 trained reservists. The Army's plans made no provisions for the National Guard, and Guardsmen returning

from the blood and mud of the Western Front were outraged. To them, the Guard had proven itself a reliable, ready instrument of national defense. Under the guiding influence of articulate, confident leaders like Maj. Gen. Milton A.

3-51 Officers of the 372d Infantry (OH, DC, CT, MD, MA, TN), 93d Division, call the roll dockside before their men board ships to return home in March 1919. They are wearing their "Blue Helmet" shoulder patches. NARA

3-52 The battle-torn colors of the 165th Infantry (formerly the 69th NY Infantry), 42d Division, are displayed on the troopship carrying the regiment home in 1919. NARA

3-53 Maj. Gen. George C. Rickards in 1921. NGEF

Reckord, the AG of Maryland, NGAUS, Guardsmen across the country pleaded their case for a rightful place as a permanent part of the military establishment. Their arguments found wide support in the states and on Capitol Hill, where legislators considered the Army's ambitious plans as too expensive and militaristic.

The National Defense Act of 1920 firmly rejected the notion of a large Regular Army backed by an immense pool of trained reserves in favor of a smaller active force reinforced by standing units of the National Guard and Organized Reservists. Congress created the "Army of the United States," a force designed to mobilize and expand in wartime around a cadre of Regulars and trained citizen-soldiers. The active Army was authorized 280,000 soldiers and assigned the missions of defending overseas possessions, expeditionary duty, and border protection. The Organized Reserves would provide a pool of officers in wartime and man nine reserve divisions to absorb and train conscripts during national emergencies. The Defense Act designated the National Guard as the first federal reserve force and set Guard strength at a maximum of 435,000 soldiers. To enhance the Guard's influence in the War Department, the chief of the Militia Bureau would be a National Guard officer. Maj. Gen. George C. Rickards of Pennsylvania was the first Guardsman to serve as chief of the Militia Bureau. (See figure 3-53.) In addition, the law stipulated that Guard officers would serve on the General Staff and established a committee of senior Guard officers to review and recommend policies affecting the entire National Guard.

## The National Guard Reconstitutes

Guardsmen left active duty at the end of World War I as individuals and not by unit. They returned home with discharge papers in hand to face an uncertain future. While the horrors of the Great War had convinced many Guardsmen to quit the military, most were determined to reform their units. In several localities, State Guard organizations created during the war controlled the armories, and state governments were slow in formulating plans to reconstitute National Guard units. However, the National Defense Act of 1920 clarified the Guard's status and established a clear direction for its rejuvenation. The act divided the United States into nine integrated corps areas with each corps containing one Regular, two National Guard, and three Reserve divisions.

As the 1920s began, Guardsmen rebuilt their units in earnest. In 1920 the Guard was a shadow of its pre–World War I strength; 56,106 soldiers filled the ranks, and fourteen states had no units at all. Within two years Guard strength was nearly 150,000, and only one state lacked Guard organization. Guard units adopted

3-54 Sgt. Gillard Thompson, Bandmaster of the 369th Infantry Band (NY) at annual training in 1924. THOMPSON

federal unit designations, and soldiers sported authorized unit crests and patches on their uniforms. (See figure 3-54.) The War Department issued standard regimental flags and company guidons. The first tanks appeared in the Guard, with one tank company assigned to each division. Guard Coast Artillery regiments took on the missions of harbor and coastal defense. By 1930 the National Guard consisted of 182,715 troops organized into twenty-two divisions supported by a federal appropriation of just under $32 million.

National Guard air units made important advances during the 1920s. The organization of each Army division called for an observation squadron for air reconnaissance missions. The first citizen-airman aviation unit formed after World War I occurred in January 1921 when Minnesota's 109th Observation Squadron became part of the 34th Division. (See figure 3-55.) A large number of Air Service pilots, crewmen, and support

3-55 One of the Curtiss "Jenny's" flown by Minnesota's 109th Observation Squadron when it received federal recognition in 1921. NGEF

3-56 Many experienced pilots joined the Guard during the 1920s such as these members of the 112th Observation Squadron (OH), 37th Division. NGEF

3-57 Like the rest of the Army in the 1930s, Guard flying units received distinctive unit insignia, such as this example on the fuselage of an O-38A flown by New York's 102d Observation Squadron. NGEF

personnel left the Army after World War I, and the National Guard was eager to take advantage of their special skills. (See figure 3-56.) Within months, Maryland and Indiana had organized their own divisional aviation units. By 1930 eighteen National Guard observation squadrons were on duty. (See figures 3-57 and 3-58.) The most dramatic accomplishment of any Guard aviator came on May 20, 1927, when Capt. Charles A. Lindbergh of Missouri's 110th Observation Squadron became the first aviator to fly solo across the hazardous North Atlantic. For his incredible passage between New York and Paris, Lindbergh received the Medal of Honor. (See figure 3-59.)

## The Great Depression

The stock market crash of October 29, 1929, set in motion an eco-

3-58 While all Air Guard units have changed missions since the 1930s, many of their patches have remained unchanged. The 116th Observation Squadron (WA) was awarded this patch in 1931, and its descendant unit, the 141st Air Refueling Wing, still wears it today. NGEF

nomic calamity that affected all Americans. Social dislocation and unemployment spread rapidly; by

3-59 Capt. Charles A. Lindbergh, was a member of Missouri's 110th Observation Squadron when he flew solo across the Atlantic Ocean in 1927. NGEF

the summer of 1932, nearly a third of the American workforce was idle. The National Guard provided stability and refuge to families and communities whose social and economic well-being were threatened. An unemployed worker who was a private in the Guard earned $75 a year by attending armory drills and summer camp. With little money available for entertainment, townspeople went to local armories for free social activities that included dances, concerts, parades, marksmanship contests, and athletic events. A number of Guard cavalry and artillery units opened their armories to make horseback riding available for families on Sundays.

The Guard earned a reputation as a reliable instrument of state power in enforcing domestic laws. On several occasions, Guard units became involved in the Great Depression's bitter labor disputes. (See figure 3-60.) During the San Francisco longshoremen's strike of July 1934, the California Guard restored order after nearly twenty-five policemen and bystanders were killed or injured in rioting. During violent protests by steelworkers in Ohio, several Guardsmen were killed, and Ohio Guard flying units dropped tear gas from the air to disperse angry crowds.

In many ways, the National Guard helped the nation to endure through the Great Depression's rigors. Armory construction, camp improvements, and government contracts to vehicle and weapons producers stimulated the economy. Many Guard units turned in their horses for new motor transport. (See figure 3-61.) Air units received

3-60 Members of the Washington Guard on state active duty during the 1935 "Lumber Workers Strike" in Tacoma. On numerous occasions during the Depression, Guardsmen in almost every state were called on to maintain order. WSHS

3-61 The last mounted color guard of Virginia's 111th Field Artillery in 1933. In the mid-1930s the National Guard's field artillery units traded their horses for trucks. VANG

## Maj. Gen. Milton A. Reckord: Service to State and Nation

Milton Atchison Reckord was an experienced veteran of two forms of combat; as a talented military leader during two world wars and as a shrewd lobbyist in Washington, D.C. He left a deep imprint on American military policy during a distinguished military career to Maryland and the nation that spanned sixty-four years.

"Milt" Reckord joined the Maryland National Guard as a private in 1901. Within two years, he was elected to company command, and in 1916 he saw duty on the Mexican Border. In World War I he commanded the 115th Infantry, 29th Division, as well as two different brigades in the division.

In 1920 General Reckord was appointed the AG of Maryland, a position he held for an unprecedented forty-five years. He mobilized Guard opinion in favor of the National Defense Act of 1920 and served as NGAUS president, 1923–25. Reckord was the author of the 1933 legislation giving Guardsmen a permanent status as both state and federal troops. General Reckord commanded the 29th Division from 1934 to 1941, and during World War II, he served as the provost marshal of the European Theater. In 1945 he helped lay the groundwork for the establishment of the postwar National Guard.

After his retirement in 1965, Reckord maintained an interest in Guard affairs. He was the first recipient of the NGAUS Distinguished Service Medal and a life member of the NGAUS Executive Council. He died in Baltimore in September 1975 at the age of ninety-five and is buried in Fallston, Maryland.

more sturdy and reliable modern aircraft capable of flying higher, faster, and farther. (See figures 3-62 and 3-63.)

### Guard Missions Defined

An important amendment to previous National Guard legislation came in 1933. Since the passage of the Dick Act thirty years earlier, the Guard's dual nature—its role as both a state and federal force—had confused and confounded many soldiers and legislators alike. Under the leadership of Milton Reckord, NGAUS, and Guard supporters drafted and passed into law legislation that defined and institutionalized the Guard's unique status.

Presented as an amendment to the National Defense Act of 1916,

3-62 Annual training for the 115th Observation Squadron (CA), 40th Division, was held at San Luis Obispo in 1935. NGEF

3-63 On the eve of World War II, the flying units of the Guard were upgraded with more modern aircraft, in this case the O-38B biplane with O-47As. NGEF

3-64 Maj. Gen. Milton Reckord. NGEF

the 1933 legislation established the "National Guard of the United States" as a permanent "reserve component" of the Army, consisting of federally recognized National Guard units. The president received the power to order these units to active duty during a national emergency. At the same time, the law identified the "National Guard of the several States" consisting of the voluntary members of the National Guard that served under the governors. In simplest terms, the "National Guard of the United States" pertained to the Guard's federal role as a reserve component of the U.S. Army, while the "National Guard of the several States" recognized the role of Guardsmen on state duty. Henceforth officers would take a dual oath to both the nation and their state. The legislation also changed the name of the Militia Bureau to the National Guard Bureau (NGB).

## The Mobilization of 1940–1941

The rising tide of Nazism and Japanese militarism threatened Europe and Asia toward the end of

the 1930s, but the majority of Americans remained staunchly isolationist. Japan's invasion of China in 1936 and Germany's attack against Poland on September 1, 1939,

3-65/3-66 Brig. Gen. Raymond S. McLain commanded the 45th "Thunderbird" Division artillery when the division was mobilized in 1940. During the war, McLain commanded the 90th Infantry Division and became the first Guardsman promoted to lieutenant general. His shoulder patch, adopted in 1923, was based on a Native American symbol of "good luck." But with the rise of Nazi Germany and its "swastika," the division changed to the "Thunderbird" still worn by members of the 45th Infantry Brigade today. NGEF converted fascist rhetoric into bellicose action. (See figures 3-65 and 3-66.) On the same day Hitler attacked Poland, General George C. Marshall became the Army's chief of staff. (See figure 3-67.) At the time, the U.S. Army, with only 190,000 Regulars, was ranked the seventeenth largest in the world, just behind the Romanian Army. President Franklin D. Roosevelt sought to enhance military readiness by increasing the Guard's annual paid drill periods from forty-eight to sixty and expanding summer camp from two to three weeks. (See figure 3-68.) Roosevelt and other political leaders assured the

country that war was not imminent, but most Americans believed that direct action against the world's rising dictators was inevitable.

Hitler's stunning defeat of France in June 1940 prompted a sharp American response. On August 27, Congress declared a

3-68 Prior to federal mobilization, many states participated in local exercises to better prepare their men for active duty. Employer support guarantees the soldier's job is safe, always a factor in Guard participation. In this period there were few laws protecting a Guardsman's job while he was on duty. NGEF

3-67 During the interwar period, many states published periodicals to give Guard members up-to-date information. When General George C. Marshall was appointed Army Chief of Staff in 1939, many in the Illinois Guard felt a special pride because he had served several years in the mid-1930s as the chief of staff of the 33d Division, composed entirely of Illinois units. NGEF

3-69 Pvt. Willis F. Ward was a member of Illinois's 184th Field Artillery when it was mobilized in 1941. Formerly the 370th Infantry, this African-American unit converted to artillery just before mobilization. NARA

3-70 The 127th Observation Squadron (KS) in formation at Wichita Municipal Airport on mobilization day, October 6, 1941. NGB

national emergency and authorized the president to call out the National Guard for one year. At the same time, Congress approved America's first peacetime draft. All males between the ages of twenty-one and thirty-five were required to register for the draft, and those selected by lottery would enter military service for one year.

On September 16, 1940, the first National Guard units were ordered to active federal service. Four Guard divisions, four observation squadrons, and eighteen coast artillery units were included in the first call-up. Between September 1940 and October 1941, over 300,000 Guardsmen in eighteen divisions, twenty-eight separate regiments, and twenty-nine observation squadrons entered federal service, doubling the size of the Army. The National Guard in 1940 lived up to its claims by functioning as America's principle reserve force

in a national emergency. (See figures 3-69 and 3-70.)

The size and speed of the mobilization created several problems. Guard units often arrived at training camps that lacked adequate billeting, mess, and training

facilities. All types of weapons and equipment were in woefully short supply. Guardsmen used stovepipes to simulate cannons and mortars, carried sticks and brooms for rifles, and pretended that pine logs were machine guns. (See figures 3-71 and

3-71 M2A1 light tanks were the mainstay of Guard tank companies upon mobilization. With signs hung on their sides, they were used in the 1941 maneuvers to represent heavier tanks. This one belongs to the 193d Tank Battalion (GA, TX, CO, AL). MEADE

3-72.) A close screening of personnel records and the implementation of new waivers against active service resulted in a mass exodus. Over 86,000 Guardsmen were released for age, medical conditions, invalid enlistments, critical job skills, and family responsibilities.

An uncertain future severely challenged Guard morale in the late spring of 1941. With America still at peace, Guardsmen wondered whether they would remain on active duty or return to civilian life. Many looked forward to going home in October. However, Hitler's invasion of the Soviet Union in June 1941 heightened tensions around the world. In Washington, D.C., General Marshall pressed Congress for an extension of the draft and Guard active duty. After divisive congressional debates, the House of Representatives on August 12 renewed conscription and the call-up of the Guard for six months by only a single vote. After passage in the Senate, the president signed the bill into law; the Guard would remain on active duty until April 1942.

A highlight of the prewar mobilization was the Army's great force-on-force maneuvers in the fall of 1941. The Guard divisions fully participated in the maneuvers in Louisiana, Tennessee, California, and the Carolinas, the largest field exercises ever conducted by American troops. The maneuvers provided valuable training for staffs and command-

3-72 Members of the 151st Infantry (IN), 38th Division, on a road march during the Louisiana Maneuvers in July 1941. **NGEF**

3-73 Missouri Guardsmen of the 203d Coast Artillery (AA) fire one of their .50 caliber antiaircraft machine guns at a target drone during the Louisiana Maneuvers in 1941. **NARA**

ers, revealed unfit leaders, and identified rising stars ready for more senior commands. (See figures 3-73 through 3-76.)

However, the renewal of the draft and the Guard mobilization by only a single vote had sent a strong signal to Japanese milita-

rists in Tokyo. Bent on expansion in the Pacific, they believed the United States would be an easy opponent; Americans apparently did not want war and had no stomach for suffering large casualties. One swift, powerful blow would surely send the Yankees

3-74 A jeep carrying men of a 44th "Four by Four" Division antitank company cross-country during the Carolina Maneuvers, November 1941. NGEF

3-76 Wearing gas masks, these men of Troop A "Essex Troop," 102d Cavalry (NJ), move through tear gas clouds during the Carolina Maneuvers, November 1941. MEADE

3-75 Like his horse-mounted forefathers this member of Troop B "Monmouth Troop," 102d Cavalry (NJ), seeks cover behind his "mount," a motorcycle instead of a horse, during the Carolina Maneuvers, November 1941. MEADE

reeling. On Thanksgiving Day 1941, as America enjoyed a traditional holiday meal, the Imperial Japanese Navy set sail from northern Japan, steaming east under a shroud of secrecy to deliver an audacious surprise attack against the American fleet at Pearl Harbor.

## The National Guard in World War II

"AIR RAID, PEARL HARBOR. THIS IS NOT A DRILL!" This short, dramatic message from Hawaii on the morning of December 7, 1941, plunged the United States into World War II. The next day President Roosevelt proclaimed December 7 as "a date which will live in infamy," and Congress declared war on Japan. In response, Germany and Italy promptly declared war on the United States. With all of the major participants finally engaged, World War II escalated to new levels of fury and destruction.

Even as Congress declared war on Japan, National Guardsmen were already in combat. When the Japanese attacked Pearl Harbor, Hawaii's 298th and 299th Infantry and the 251st Coast Artillery from California took part in the defense of Oahu and fired the National Guard's first shots of World War II. In November 1941 three Guard units with troops from seven states had arrived in the Philippines to bolster the island's defenses. The largest was New Mexico's 200th Coast Artillery, consisting of 1,800

3-77 Members of New Mexico's 200th Coast Artillery (AA) man a position at Clark Field in January 1942. NGEF

3-78 On December 26, 1941, a tank from Company C, 194th Tank Battalion (CA), attacked a Japanese roadblock and destroyed two artillery positions as the company tried to halt the enemy advance toward Manila. NGB

men, many of them Hispanic. (See figure 3-77.) During the 1940 mobilization, the Army had consolidated the tank companies assigned to each Guard division into four composite tank battalions. The 192d Tank Battalion, with troops from Wisconsin, Illinois, Ohio, and Kentucky, and the 194th Tank Battalion, consisting of companies from Minnesota and California, with a sprinkling of Guardsmen from Missouri, added their firepower to the Philippine defenses. The 200th Coast Artillery valiantly defended against Japanese aerial attacks at Clark Field near Manila on December 8. During the battle, the New Mexicans fired the first shots in defense of the Philippines and suffered a number of casualties while downing five enemy planes. The Japanese Army invaded the Philippines, backing the Americans and Filipinos onto the Bataan Peninsula and the island fortress of Corregidor. Cut off from supplies and reinforcements, the defenders held out for four months. Throughout the defensive battles, Guard units fought stubbornly. (See figure 3-78.) Finally, with their backs to the sea and low on all commodities except courage, the "Battling Bastards of Bataan" surrendered on April 9, 1942. (See figure 3-79.) The defenders suffered through the horrors of the Bataan "Death March" and went on to endure over three years of deprivations and brutality in Japanese prisoner of war camps. (See figure 3-80.)

While fighting raged in the Philippines, Guardsmen at home prepared for combat. Air units trained at various installations throughout the United States. (See figures 3-81 and 3-82.) Hitler's blitzkrieg victories convinced the Army of the effectiveness of maneuver warfare and prompted the abandonment of the square infantry division as the primary combat formation. Earlier in 1941 the Army had created a "triangular division" based on the employment of three infantry regiments, and active duty divisions converted to the new design. Stripped of all unnecessary units, the smaller triangular division was designed for agility and responsiveness on the fluid battlefields of mechanized warfare. After Pearl Harbor, the Army directed the Guard divisions to convert from the square to the triangular configuration. The end result of the reorganization was to release eighteen infantry regiments for duty elsewhere. (See figure 3-83.) A few of the separate regiments went on to fight with Regular or draftee divisions, but most assumed security missions at various locations worldwide.

The outbreak of war precipitated other changes in the states and at NGB. The Guard mobilization left the governors without troops, and as in World War I, the states created State Guard forces. Throughout the war, State Guards performed disaster relief, aid to civil authorities, and security missions. Overall control of the State Guards fell to NGB, and at their

3-79 Among the "Battling Bastards of Bataan" were nearly 2,000 Guardsmen of the 200th Coast Artillery and the 192d and 194th Tank Battalions. NARA

3-80 The "Bataan Medal" was issued by New Mexico to each member of the 200th Coast Artillery for their duty in the Philippines at the start of World War II. It was presented to the veterans or the next of kin of those who died in service, in a special ceremony on December 7, 1946. NGEF

3-81 A flight crew of the 105th Observation Squadron (TN) go through a preflight briefing before taking off on an antisubmarine patrol along the East Coast from their base at Langley Field, VA, April 1942.

3-82 Members of New York's 102d Observation Squadron stand in front of the unit's only C-45A cargo carrier while stationed at Ontario, CA, in May 1942. The unit flew their O-47s on antisubmarine patrols along the California coast. NGEF

3-83 The 176th Infantry Band (VA) plays during a ceremony at Fort Benning, GA, in 1944. This regiment was one of eighteen separated when the Guard divisions were "triangularized" in 1942. It served first as part of the garrison of Washington, D.C., and then in 1943 moved to Benning, where its experienced soldiers taught new draftees basic training skills. VANG

3-84 Troops of the "Americal" Infantry Division board ships in New Caledonia to sail for Guadalcanal in October 1942. NARA

peak strength in June 1943, the State Guards numbered 170,403 troops in forty-four states. With all National Guard units on active duty during the war, NGB's authority was greatly diminished. In March 1942 NGB ceased to exist as a special staff and came under the authority of the Army's AG. Before the end of the war, the NGB staff was reduced to forty-nine civilian workers, who served as a subordinate agency of the Personnel Division of the Army Service Forces.

A Japanese whirlwind overran Southeast Asia and the central Pacific in early 1942. The miraculous victory at Midway in May 1942 gave the United States the strategic initiative, but the Japanese continued to occupy key terrain. Japanese forces in New Guinea and in the Solomon Islands threatened Australia and the sea routes linking Australia and Hawaii. National Guard infantry was at the center of early American victories on Guadalcanal and in New Guinea. Three infantry regiments—the 132d (Illinois), 164th (North Dakota), and the 182d (Massachusetts)— made available by the triangular division conversion were rushed to New Caledonia in March 1942. The three regiments, as well as Guard artillery and support troops, formed the basis for the activation of the "Americal" Division on May 27, 1942, the nineteenth Guard division to serve in World War II. ("Americal" is an abbreviation of "America" and "New Caledonia.") The 164th Infantry deployed to Guadalcanal in October to reinforce U.S. Marines. (See figure 3-84.) The North Dakotans became the first Army troops to go on the offensive in World War II. The remainder of the division soon arrived on the island and played a major role in the Japanese defeat. For its actions on Guadalcanal, the Americal Division became the only Army division to be awarded the Navy Presidential Unit Citation. In the last stages of the Guadalcanal campaign, Ohio's 37th Division entered the fight and saw action in April 1943.

The 32d Division from Wisconsin and Michigan was set to deploy to Europe when it received orders to head for the port of embarkation at San Francisco. By May 1942 the "Red Arrow" Division was in Australia, and before the end of the summer, it was in New Guinea fighting alongside the Australians. General Douglas MacArthur ordered the 32d Division to take Buna, a critical Japanese enclave on the northern tip of New Guinea. In one of the most grueling campaigns of the war, Guardsmen attacked heavily defended Japanese pillboxes in the thick, sweltering jungles. Short on supplies, troops ate half rations and suffered through bouts of malaria. The Americans absorbed crippling losses but finally captured Buna in January 1943. The 41st Division, manned by Guardsmen from the Pacific Northwest, relieved the 32d Division on New Guinea, and the Red Arrow Division returned to Australia for rest and refit. (See figures 3-85, 3-86, and 3-87.)

**3-85 Men of the 128th Infantry (WI), 32d Infantry Division, rest and eat during their advance to Oro Baya, New Guinea, in November 1942. NARA**

## The War in Europe

Though American naval and ground forces in the Pacific were battling the Japanese with positive results, the priority for operations shifted to Europe. In consultation with the Allies, the Roosevelt Administration determined that Nazi Germany posed a more serious threat than Japan and adopted a national strategy of "Germany First." Initially, General Marshall and the Joint Chiefs of Staff (JCS) advocated a direct attack against Nazi-occupied Western Europe across the English Channel from bases in Great Britain. However, it soon became evident that American troops were not yet ready for such an ambitious undertaking. President Roosevelt insisted that American troops engage the Germans before the end of 1942 and decided to support Allied operations in the Mediterranean.

For American troops, the road to Berlin would begin in the sands of North Africa.

During 1942–43, Guardsmen were in the thick of the fighting in the Mediterranean. The 34th Infantry Division was the first American combat division to deploy overseas following Pearl Harbor. The "Red Bull" Division sailed to Ireland in January 1942 to train for the invasion of Western Europe. Reflecting Allied strategic decisions, the 34th Division was reassigned to the landing forces for Operation TORCH, the invasion of North Africa. On November 8, 1942, the 34th Division made an assault landing on the Algerian coast and, with other U.S. divisions, fought its way across the sands and mountains of Tunisia against Germany's Afrika Korps. The enemy surrendered in May 1943,

with the 34th Division suffering 4,200 casualties.

The 45th Division had its baptism of fire on June 8, 1943, during the amphibious invasion of Sicily. (See figure 3-88.) In twenty-two days of continuous combat, the "Thunderbird" Division covered more ground than any other Army division. (See figure 3-89.) The 36th Division from Texas became the third Guard division to see action in the Mediterranean when it landed at Salerno on the Italian peninsula on September 9, 1943. Stiff enemy resistance nearly doomed

3-87 The "Red Arrow" shoulder patch of the 32d Infantry Division was adopted in World War I. It represents the division "piercing the Hindenburg Line (indicated by the bar) like an arrow." It's currently worn by members of the 32d Infantry Brigade (WI). NGEF

3-86 Three members of Service Company, 127th Infantry (WI), 32d Division, move supplies by water during the Buna campaign, December 1942. This proved the fastest way to resupply forward areas given the heavy jungles of New Guinea. NARA

3-88 Soldiers of the 45th Infantry Division land in Sicily on June 8, 1943. NARA

3-89 Oklahoma Guardsman Sgt. Bill Mauldin started drawing cartoon "GIs" for the 45th Division newspaper while serving in Sicily. His "Willy and Joe" series proved so popular that he was soon transferred to the staff of the Army-run daily newspaper *Stars and Stripes*. His characters appeared for more than two years, bringing a small bit of cheer to frontline troops serving all over Europe. NGEF

3-90 Troops of the 34th Infantry Division drive a DUKW amphibious truck onto the beach south of Naples near Agropoli, Italy, on September 21, 1943. They would be in the Po Valley of northern Italy at war's end in May 1945. NARA

the landing, and the 45th Division quickly deployed into the Salerno beachhead to strengthen the Allied defenses. The invaders finally captured Naples and began a slow, bloody advance up the Italian peninsula despite rugged, mountainous terrain, abysmal weather, and a determined enemy. The 34th, 36th, and 45th Divisions participated in every major campaign in Italy, including the assault of the German Winter Line, the bloody crossing of the Rapido River, desperate fighting at Anzio, and the liberation of Rome on June 5, 1944. (See figures 3-90 through 3-93.)

On June 6, 1944, Allied land, sea, and air forces invaded Western Europe in the largest amphibious assault in military history. After airborne landings and preparatory bombardments by air and naval forces, Allied ground troops assaulted five separate invasion beaches in Normandy. The most difficult fighting occurred on Omaha Beach, where elements of the 1st and 29th Infantry Divisions

3-91 Corp. Joe Digatona, a Guard member of Minneapolis's 151st Field Artillery Battalion, 34th Division, calls in a fire mission during the Cassino campaign in Italy, January 1944. NARA

3-92 1st Lt. Ernest Childers, a Creek Indian and mobilized Guardsman in the 45th Infantry Division, is being congratulated by Lt. Gen. Jacob Devers on July 13, 1944. He was awarded the Medal of Honor for wiping out two machine gun nests during the Italian campaign. **NARA**

3-93 As the focus of the war moved to Normandy, France, following the D-Day invasion in June 1944, men of the 34th Division were still fighting their way up the Italian "boot." They captured Pisa on July 23, 1944. **NARA**

landed abreast. German defenses, high bluffs, and rough seas made the assault precarious. By the end of the day, the divisions had a viable toehold on the French coastline. The 29th Division went on to accumulate an impressive combat record in Europe, though at a high cost. Veterans grimly recalled that in reality three separate 29th Divisions existed during the war; one on the front lines, one in the hospital, and one in the cemetery. (See figure 3-94, 3-95, and 3-96.)

Meanwhile, the Allies landed in southern France on August 15, 1944, to increase pressure on Nazi forces. Both the 36th and 45th Divisions splashed ashore in the French Riviera, were at the

3-94 The 29th "Blue and Gray" Infantry Division was stationed for eighteen months in England preparing for the invasion of France. While training there, the division organized the "29th Ranger Battalion" to give intensive training to a select number of its men. The battalion's training was featured in an issue of *Yank* magazine. It was inactivated and its men returned to their former units before the invasion. **VANG**

3-95 Two members of Company E, 116th Infantry (VA), 29th Division, standing under the cover of the chalk cliffs in the 1st Division area on D-Day. Several of Company E's landing craft were pulled off course by strong currents, putting their men on the wrong beach. **NARA**

3-96 By D+1 members of the 175th Infantry (MD), 29th Division, were able to walk ashore without encountering enemy fire. They are wearing assault gas masks on their chests and floatation belts around their waists. **NARA**

3-97 Medics from the 36th "Texas" Infantry Division treat wounded civilians behind an M-4 Sherman "DD" (swimming tank) near San Raphael, French Riviera, August 15, 1944. **NARA**

forefront of the offensive up the Rhone River valley, and fought their way through to the German frontier. (See figures 3-97 and 3-98.)

Five other National Guard divisions proved their mettle in Europe. The 30th Division arrived in Normandy ten days after D-Day and went on to a stellar combat career. At the battle of Mortain, the "Old Hickory" Division blunted a strong German counter-attack intended to thwart the American breakout from Normandy and in the fall of 1944 was one of the first American divisions to breach the vaunted Siegfried Line. (See figures 3-99

3-98 Troops of the 45th Division make their fourth beach assault landing of the war when they invade southern France on the Riviera, August 15, 1944. **NARA**

3-99 Getting their first hot meal in days, these men of Company G, 117th Infantry (NC), 30th Infantry Division, have just come off the line near Bult, France, November 12, 1944. NARA

3-100 Having just crossed over into Germany, members of the 30th Division move through Setterich on November 19, 1944. NARA

and 3-100.) The 35th Division received its baptism of fire in Normandy while helping to capture the vital road junction at St. Lo in July 1944. (See figure 3-101.) After Lt. Gen. George S. Patton's dash across France, the "Santa Fe" Division liberated the city of Nancy, took part in the American offensive following the Battle of the Bulge, and ended the war on the banks of the Elbe River. (See figures 3-102, 3-103, and 3-104.) The 28th Division helped to liberate Paris but stumbled badly during the ill-fated attack against the small town of Schmidt in the Huertgen Forest. (See figure 3-105.) Because of punishing casualties, veterans referred to the division's red, keystone shoulder patch as "the bloody bucket." After a period of rest and retraining, the 28th Division redeemed its reputation during a series of stubborn defensive battles in the opening days of the battle of the Bulge. (See figure 3-106.) The 26th Division entered combat in Lorraine in the late summer of 1944 and led the advance to capture the fortress complex at Metz. In December the "Yankee" Division participated in Patton's

3-101 Soldiers of the 35th "Santa Fe" Infantry Division move through the ruins of St. Lo, France, in July 1944. NARA

3-102 A machine gun section of Company H, 134th Infantry (NE), fighting on the outskirts of Lutrebois, Luxembourg, January 1945. NGEF

3-103 Pvt. Steve Jackson, of the 137th Infantry (KS), 35th Division, stands guard while occupying Lutrebois, Luxembourg, January 6, 1945. NARA

3-104 Medics of the 110th Medical Battalion (NE), 35th Division, evacuate wounded soldiers of the 134th Infantry from Lutrebois, Luxembourg, January 6, 1945. NENG

attack to relieve the hard-pressed defenders at Bastogne. (See figure 3-107.) The 26th Division drove across Germany the following spring, captured Linz, Austria, and ended the war in Czechoslovakia. (See figure 3-108.) The 44th Division did not arrive in Europe until October 1944 and fought in the difficult Vosges Mountains. In the last months of the war, the "Four by Four" Division breached the Siegfried Line, captured Mannheim, and

3-105 Men of the 28th Infantry Division march past the Arch de Triumph and down the Champs Elysees, Paris, marking the city's liberation, August 29, 1944. They immediately resumed combat operations after the parade. NARA

3-106 Pvt. James Wheeler, Quartermaster Company, 28th Division, attaches snowshoes to make walking through the deep drifts a bit easier, Ban de Laveline, France, January 28, 1945. NARA

3-107 The 26th Infantry Division led the advance of Lt. Gen. George Patton's relief force to lift the siege of Bastogne, Belgium, December 24, 1944. NARA

3-108 Soldiers of the 101st Infantry (MA), 26th Division, cross the Schedlt River in Germany in March 1945. This is one of the Guard's oldest units, dating from 1636. NARA

3-109 Members of the Antitank Company, 114th Infantry (NJ), 44th "Four by Four" Infantry Division, relax around a fire in the ruins of Lanueville, France, November 16, 1944. NARA

3-110 Two soldiers from the Military Police Company, 44th Division, check German prisoners of war for contraband before moving them to a rear area, Sabrebourg, France, November 22, 1944. NARA

ended the war in Austria. (See figures 3-109 and 3-110.) Several Guard infantry regiments reassigned by the divisional reorganizations of 1942 also fought in Europe as part of other Army divisions. (See figure 3-111.)

The three Guard divisions that had first entered combat in the Mediterranean fought on to the war's end. The 36th and 45th Divisions helped to overrun Germany in the spring of 1945. (See figures 3-112, 3-113, and 3-114.) Meanwhile, the 34th Division continued fighting in northern Italy until German forces surrendered there on May 2, 1945. Altogether, the nine National Guard divisions that served in Europe suffered total losses of 125,630.

3-111 A mortar team from Company D, 121st Infantry (GA), fires a round during the 8th Infantry Division's assault across the Roer River, Brandenburg, Germany, December 7, 1944. The 121st, being separated from its assignment with the 31st Division in 1942, was assigned to the 8th Division and saw combat with it throughout the war. NARA

3-112 Headquarters of the 142d Infantry (TX), 36th Division, in Schveigen, Germany, sports a new Texas flag sent to the regiment by the state's governor, March 22, 1945. NARA

3-113 Infantrymen of the 142d Infantry catch a lift on an M-10 tank destroyer entering Bergzaborn, Germany, March 23, 1945. NARA

Compared to World War I, black Guardsmen saw little combat in World War II. The War Department failed to address racial inequality in the military and supported policies of segregation and discrimination. Black Guard units that had served with distinction in 1917–18 were mostly converted to artillery and engineer units. New York's 369th Infantry became the 369th Antiaircraft Gun Battalion that garrisoned Hawaii and ended the war as part of the occupation forces on Okinawa. The only black Guard units to see combat were the 1698th and 1699th Engineer Battalions (Combat) that were formed from Illinois's 370th Infantry and saw action in Europe near the end of the war. Only the 372d Infantry retained its original organization throughout the war while performing guard missions in the New York City area. In early 1945, the 372d shipped out to Hawaii and served as a garrison there until January 1946.

National Guard flying units and pilots contributed to the war effort. After Pearl Harbor, Guardsmen flew antisubmarine patrols along both coasts. The Army Air Forces (AAF) were desperately short of trained pilot instructors, and eight National Guard squadrons spent the entire war in stateside training camps. Many Guard pilots had more flight experience than AAF aviators, and numbers of Guardsmen were transferred to command positions in AAF units. (See figure 3-115.)

3-114 Members of the Military Police Company, 45th Division, are shocked as they examine one of more than 100 railcars filled with dead bodies of inmates from the Dachau concentration camp. The 45th was one of the first American units to liberate this extermination camp, Dachau, Germany, April 1945. NARA

3-115 Lt. Col. Addison Baker, who entered active duty with Ohio's 112th Observation Squadron, was a group leader on the bomber raid over the Ploesti oil fields in Romania in August 1943. Despite crippling damage to his plane, he continued to lead his group to target. His bomber soon crashed, with all crewmen killed. He was awarded the Medal of Honor for his heroic leadership. NGB

3-116 "Chicken Little," a P-51 Mustang fighter modified for photographic reconnaissance, is prepared for its next mission by Minnesota's 109th Tactical Reconnaissance Squadron (formerly the 109th Obs Sq), England, 1944. NGB

Three of the first observation squadrons to depart the United States were the 111th (Texas), 122d (Louisiana), and the 154th (Arkansas). They sailed for the Mediterranean as part of the 68th Observation Group and took part in the invasion of North Africa. Other squadrons that saw early combat were Michigan's 107th Observation Squadron and the 109th from Minnesota. (See figure 3-116.) Redesignated as tactical reconnaissance squadrons, the two units flew photoreconnaissance missions over Normandy as a prelude to the D-Day invasion. In July 1944 the 107th became the first AAF unit to operate from French soil. (See figure 3-117.)

## The War in the Pacific

While Allied operations in Europe focused ultimately on the invasion of Western Europe and the occupation of Nazi Germany, American strategy in the Pacific sought to isolate Japan geographically as a prelude to the actual invasion of the home islands. After the initial operations on Guadalcanal and New Guinea in 1942, the availability of Navy and Marine forces ensured that the United States would maintain pressure against Japan even while implementing a "Germany First" strategy. The main objective of all operations was to strangle Japan's economy and make the home islands vulnerable to direct attack by occupying a triangle formed by Formosa, China, and the Philippines. A strategy finally emerged that employed dual

3-117 Landing Strip A-9 in Normandy, France, July 1944. Used by aircraft of the 107th Tactical Reconnaissance Squadron (MI), its close location to the fighting front allowed for quick air support. NGB

offensives directed westward across the Pacific's vast reaches. In the Southwest Pacific, General MacArthur would command U.S. and Australian divisions, with supporting air and naval forces, in attacks aimed at recapturing the Philippines. In the Central Pacific, Adm. Chester W. Nimitz would attack with considerable naval forces as well as Marine and Army divisions. Nimitz's goals were to destroy the Japanese Navy, capture island airfields that would allow the strategic air bombardment of Japan, and place ground forces within reach of the Japanese home islands.

Throughout the Pacific campaigns, the National Guard contributed ten divisions that played an important role in Japan's final defeat. New York's 27th Infantry Division was the only Guard outfit to support Nimitz's Central Pacific drive, but its combat role had

several significant outcomes. Sent to Hawaii in March 1942, the 27th Division formed regimental combat teams that participated in Nimitz's opening blows. While the Marine Corps attacked Tarawa in November 1943, the 27th Division seized nearby Makin Island after three days of combat. (See figure 3-118.) Only three months later, the 27th captured Eniwetok in the Marshall Islands. In both instances, Marine commanders criticized the Army's cautious tactics and complained of poor leadership and inadequate training in the 27th Division.

The Army-Marine confrontation came to a head during fighting on Saipan in the Marianas Islands in June 1944. (See figure 3-119.) Dissatisfied with the 27th Division's conduct during some of the most vicious fighting yet encountered in the island campaigns, the Marine Corps general in overall command of the invasion force relieved the 27th's commander, a Regular Army general. The relief initiated bitter recriminations between marines and soldiers that had repercussions far beyond Saipan's shores. The incident poisoned Army and Marine Corps relations for the remainder of the war and fueled interservice rivalry afterward. After Saipan, the 27th Division participated in the bloody capture of Okinawa and was preparing for the invasion of Japan when the war ended. The division suffered 6,800 battle casualties, but its most enduring legacy from the war occurred on Saipan. The roots of the uneasy rivalry that has existed between the Army and the Marine Corps since World War II can be traced to the relief of the 27th Division's commander on Saipan.

Nine Guard divisions played a key role in MacArthur's Southwest Pacific campaigns that traversed the mountainous jungles of New

3-118 Men of the 165th Infantry (NY), 27th "Empire" Infantry Division, wade ashore on "Yellow Beach Two" on Makin Atoll in the Gilbert Island group, November 20, 1943. NARA

3-120 Members of the 43d "Winged Victory" Infantry Division load supplies in preparation to depart Guadalcanal in July 1943. They would soon invade the Northern Solomon Islands, securing Munda Airfield. NARA

3-119 Lt. Col. William O'Brien, commander of 1st Battalion, 105th Infantry (NY), 27th Division, briefs his company commanders on Ridge 300, Saipan, July 19, 1944. NGEF

3-121 Soldiers of the 145th Infantry (OH), 37th "Buckeye" Infantry Division, unload supplies on Bougainville, November 19, 1943. NARA

3-122 Artillerymen of the 136th Field Artillery (OH), 37th Division, celebrate Christmas in Bougainville, 1943. NARA

3-123 Medics with the 124th Infantry (FL), 31st "Dixie" Infantry Division, move along a jungle path in their advance on Aitape Island, New Guinea, July 31, 1944. NARA

3-124 A bulldozer of the 106th Engineer Combat Battalion (MS), 31st Division, clears a path through the jungle to lay out an encampment site, Morotai Island, New Guinea, September 17, 1944. NARA

3-125 Men of 1st Battalion, 124th Infantry, 31st Division, take a break in a native village during their advance across Morotai Island, New Guinea, September 17, 1944. NARA

Guinea and liberated the Philippines. During the last half of 1943, the 37th, 40th, 43d and Americal Divisions fought in the Solomon Islands. (See figure 3-120.) Fighting raged in New Georgia and Bougainville, and American troops eliminated the Japanese bastion at Rabaul. (See figures 3-121 and 3-122.) Starting in early 1944, MacArthur conducted a brilliant air, land, and sea offensive along the northern coast of New Guinea. Superior mobility allowed American forces either to bypass completely enemy strongpoints or to concentrate overwhelming combat power against isolated Japanese defenses. The 31st, 33d, 41st, and 43d Divisions saw action at Aitape, Hollandia, Wakde, and Biak, sometimes hitting together and at other times striking singly against more distant targets. (See figures 3-123 through 3-128.) By September 1944, MacArthur's forces were well

3-126 An "Alligator" tracked amphibious landing craft brings men of the 186th Infantry (OR), 41st "Sunset" Infantry Division, ashore on Lake Santani, New Guinea, April 24, 1944. NARA

3-127 "Hitting the beach" on Wakde Island in Dutch New Guinea are members of the 163d Infantry (OR), 41st Division, on May 18, 1944. NARA

3-128 A machine gun crew of the 41st Division prepares to meet a Japanese counterattack on Biak Island, August 30, 1944. NARA

3-129 Soldiers of Company D, 185th Infantry (CA), 40th "Sunshine" Infantry Division, man a defensive position during the American invasion of Paney Island, Philippines, March 18, 1945. NARA

3-130 Engineers of the 115th Engineer Combat Battalion, 40th Division, remove a bomb planted by retreating Japanese to booby trap a bridge on Negros Island, Philippines, March 29, 1945. NARA

3-131 Under heavy enemy machine gunfire, men of the 41st Division crouch low in a bomb crater on Jolo Island, Philippines, April 1945. NARA

**3-132** For the first time since the fall of the Philippines, newly liberated American civilian prisoners of the Santo Tomas Internment Camp, Manila, raise the American flag on February 6, 1945. They were freed by the 37th Division as it moved into Manila. **NARA**

**3-134** Men of Company I, 103d Infantry (CT), 43d Division, advance up the slopes of Mount Tanauan, Luzon, Philppines, March 21, 1945. **NARA**

**3-133** Gen. Douglas MacArthur joins American soldiers in raising the flag again over the parade ground of the fortress of Corregidor, Philippines, March 2, 1945. **NARA**

toward Singapore and the southern tip of the Philippines.

With the Navy's successes in the Central Pacific, MacArthur received permission to carry out his return to the Philippines. In November 1944, the 32d and Americal Divisions landed on Leyte followed not long afterward by the 31st and 41st Divisions. After the Leyte invasion, MacArthur planned major attacks on Luzon and Mindanao. The 31st and 41st Divisions landed on Mindanao in early 1945, and the 40th Division soon joined them. By late summer, American forces had entirely surrounded the last defenders on the island. (See figures 3-129, 3-130, and 3-131.) Four Guard divisions—the 32d, 37th, 40th, and 43d—were in the vanguard of MacArthur's main blow against Luzon. The offensive slashed through Luzon's lowlands to

capture Manila in the Army's most difficult urban fighting of the entire war. (See figure 3-132.) Meanwhile, the 38th Division landed on the Bataan Peninsula and recaptured Corregidor. (See figure 3-133.) Facing defeat, the Japanese withdrew into northern Luzon for a characteristic last stand. The 33d, 37th, and 38th Divisions plunged northward into the tropical mountains to defeat the Japanese and complete the conquest of the Philippines. (See figures 3-134 through 3-138.)

Seven National Guard observation squadrons fought in the Pacific. Two squadrons, the 106th (Alabama) and the 110th (Missouri), fought in the southwestern Pacific Theater. The 106th flew from Henderson Field on Guadalcanal in July 1943. The 110th flew reconnaissance missions out of New Guinea, the Philippines, and

3-135 Soldiers of the 130th Infantry (IL), 33d "Prairie" Infantry Division move through the ruins of Baguio City, Luzon, Philippines, April 27, 1945. NARA

3-136 A 57mm gun of the Antitank Company, 152d Infantry (IN), 38th "Cyclone" Infantry Division, in action at Marakina, Luzon, Philippines, May 11, 1945. NARA

3-137 A battery of 105mm howitzers of the 122d Field Artillery (IL), 33d Division, pound Japanese positions near Butac, Luzon, Philippines, June 10, 1945. NARA

3-138 While fighting continued to rage in the Philippines, American forces, including elements of the 37th Division, landed on the island of Iwo Jima in April 1945. Pvt. Ernest Callison of the 147th Infantry (OH) takes a break to read a letter from home. NARA

Okinawa. (See figure 3-139.) Five National Guard squadrons saw action in the China-Burma-India Theater, performing photoreconnaissance missions over Burma's mountainous jungles and flying observation, light transport, and evacuation missions for British, Chinese, and American troops. (See figure 3-140.)

The ten Guard divisions in the Pacific bore a significant portion of the burden of Army operations while suffering 48,521 casualties.

Combat losses and disease depleted the numbers of Guardsmen in the ranks, but many of the divisions

3-139 As the end of the war approached, many units started assessing their combat record. This sign boasts that Missouri's 110th Tactical Reconnaissance Squadron accounted for at least 123 enemy aircraft destroyed either on the ground or in aerial combat. NGEF

3-141 Maj. Gen. Robert S. Beightler. NGEF

3-140 The one theater of the war in which the Guard played only a small role was China-Burma-India. Only one Army Guard and five Air units were involved, including the 115th Tactical Reconnaissance Squadron (CA), flying Stinson L-5 light scout planes, May 1945. NGB

(See figure 3-141.) In addition, the 37th Division's principle staff officers were Guardsmen, and most infantry regiments had Guard commanders. Compared to outfits in Europe, where casualties were significantly higher, Guard divisions in the Pacific better retained their state and regional identities.

Preparations for the invasion of Japan came to an abrupt halt after the atomic bombings of Hiroshima and Nagasaki. World War II ended with Japanese surrender ceremonies aboard the battleship USS *Missouri* in Tokyo Bay on September 2, 1945. Though the troops thought only of returning home, several Guard divisions remained in the Philippines and in Japan on occupation duty. (See figures 3-142, 3-143, and 3-144.) The 40th Division went to Korea to

retained a Guard flavor in terms of leadership style and command positions. An Ohio Guardsman, Maj. Gen. Robert S. Beightler, commanded the 37th Division for all of World War II and retained Guard officers as the chief of staff and division artillery commander.

3-142 Members of the Military Police Company, 38th Division guard Japanese prisoners on Luzon after the Japanese surrender ending the war, September 17, 1945. NARA

3-143 Men of the 33d Division aboard a train in Honshu, Japan, on their way to occupation duty, September 25, 1945. NARA

3-144 Soldiers of the 182d Infantry (MA), Americal Division receive medals in Japan just prior to their returning to the United States for discharge. NGEF

3-145 Sgt. Joseph Richards, 160th Infantry (CA), 40th Division, checks the rice ration of a Japanese soldier for contraband before allowing him to board a ship for home, October 1945. The 40th Division performed occupation duties in Korea after the war. NARA

3-147 The National Guard Memorial in Honolulu, Hawaii. DOUBLER

assist in the repatriation of Japanese prisoners. (See figure 3-145.) In April 1946 the "Sunshine" Division was the last Guard division released from active duty.

National Guard ground and air units, and the over 300,000 citizen-soldiers who manned them, were integral to America's victory in World War II. The Guard divisions were a ready, standing force that deployed immediately, and without them, America's initial ground response might have taken years instead of months. The National Guard divisions bore their share of the fighting, often leading the way or battling alongside Regular Army and reserve divisions. The National Guard Memorial at the Vierville Draw (figure 3-146), where the 29th Infantry Division landed on Omaha Beach, and a commemorative plaque in the National Memorial Cemetery of the Pacific in Honolulu (figure 3-147) stand as permanent reminders of the National Guard's service in Europe and the Pacific during World War II.

3-146 The National Guard Memorial in Normandy, France. NGEF

# FOUR

# The Army National Guard, 1946–2006

## The Guard Rebuilds after World War II

As World War II ended, the War Department formulated plans for the postwar armed forces without full consideration of the National Guard. Under the leadership of a new president, Maj. Gen. Ellard A. Walsh, NGAUS became the focal point for efforts to restore the postwar Guard. Small in stature but vigorous in action, Walsh never missed an opportunity to speak out on the Guard's behalf. (See figure 4-1.) To make the Guard's voice heard more effectively, he established a small, full-time staff for the association, began planning for a NGAUS headquarters building in Washington, D.C., and started publication of a magazine. Walsh served as NGAUS president until 1957. When he left office, Walsh considered federal funding for armory construction and retirement benefits for long-serving Guardsmen as his greatest accomplishments. (See figures 4-2 and 4-3.)

As a result of negotiations between NGAUS and the War Department, General Marshall agreed that following World War II the Guard should resume its traditional place in national defense. The War Department issued a directive in October 1945 outlining the Guard's purpose, mission, and force structure. The National Guard would remain an integral part of America's first line of defense and retain its unique status as both a state and federal force. The National Guard received approval to organize as many as 425,000 soldiers into twenty-seven divisions, twenty-one regimental combat teams, and hundreds of other separate companies and battalions. Starting in the summer of 1946, the Guard's reorganization was rapid and widespread. By the end of 1948, 288,427 Army Guardsmen were

4-1   Maj. Gen. Ellard Walsh. NGEF

4-2   The 1959 National Guard Association Memorial in Washington, D.C. NGEF

formed into 4,646 units, and within two years, the Army Guard reached a peak strength of nearly 325,000 soldiers. Twenty-one states and the territory of Hawaii had completed their Guard reorganizations by 1950. (See figures 4-4 and 4-5.)

Near the end of the war, the United States took the lead in founding the United Nations (UN) and became a key player in that global organization. In subsequent years, the UN became a forum for assembling coalitions against various security threats. Other significant changes to America's defense establishment occurred. The National Security Act of 1947 completely reorganized America's armed forces by creating the position of Secretary of Defense and three military departments, the Army, Navy, and newly formed Air Force. On October 1, 1948, the modern NGB headquarters came into being. The Chief, NGB (CNGB), retained a staff to coordinate legislative, public affairs, budget, and administrative functions. Army and Air Divisions, both under the direction of National Guard major generals, handled all matters for the Army National Guard (ARNG) and the Air National Guard (ANG). Legislation in 1949 created the Department of Defense (DOD), and in that same year, the Allied powers banded together to form the North Atlantic Treaty Organization (NATO), a collective security arrangement to deter Soviet

4-3 The new National Guard Memorial, also in Washington, D.C., was dedicated in 1991. NGEF

4-4 In the early Cold War period, the Guard used World War II equipment, like this M-4 tank of the 190th Tank Battalion (GA). NGEF

4-5 Newer equipment, like this Stinson L-19 used for artillery observation, came into Guard service in the mid-1950s. NGEF

4-6 The 272d Field Artillery Battalion (MA) passes in review soon after entering active duty during the Korean War. This unit was one of six all African American units mobilized. LISTMAN

4-7 A 90mm antiaircraft gun of New Mexico's 716th Anti-aircraft Artillery Battalion trains at Fort Bliss, TX, after mobilization. PERKINS

4-8 Capt. Audie Murphy, America's most decorated soldier from World War II, joined the Texas National Guard during the Korean War. His image was used as a recruiting tool for the Guard. TXMM

aggression against western Europe.

## The Korean War, 1950–1953

On June 25, 1950, North Korea launched a sudden, massive invasion against South Korea. Within days, President Harry S. Truman, the former Guardsman from Missouri, committed American forces as part of a broader UN effort. The United States rushed reinforcements to Korea, but by late summer, the North Koreans had backed American and South Korean troops into a defensive perimeter surrounding the southern port city of Pusan.

On July 19, President Truman announced a partial mobilization of Guardsmen for twenty-one months. The first ARNG units ordered to active service reported to their armories on August 14. In August and September 1950, thousands of Army Guardsmen reported for duty. The lion's share of soldiers came from four infantry divisions; the 28th (Pennsylvania), the 40th (California), the 45th (Oklahoma), and the 43d (Connecticut, Rhode Island, and Vermont). In addition, hundreds of separate combat, combat support, and combat service support units were mobilized. By the summer of 1951, nearly 110,000 ARNG soldiers were on active duty. (See figures 4-6, 4-7, and 4-8.) Many units lost over half of their most experienced personnel, who were rushed to Korea as individual replacements to serve in Regular Army outfits. The wholesale loss of seasoned soldiers severely tested Guard morale, and a significant number of Guardsmen served in Korea as individuals rather than as members in Guard units.

A significant number of units deployed quickly to Korea. The first Guard unit to reach South

4-9 A soldier of New York's 955th Field Artillery Battalion watches the Korean skies for enemy aircraft from an M-3 half track mounting a quad .50-caliber "Sky Sweeper" antiaircraft gun. NGEF

4-10 Arkansas's 937th Field Artillery Battalion digs in a 155mm self-propelled "Long Tom" howitzer in Korea, 1951. Redesignated as the 142d FA, this unit saw combat in the Persian Gulf. NGEF

Korea was the 231st Transportation Truck Battalion from Baltimore, Maryland, one of the Guard's all-black units. The 231st reached Pusan on New Year's Day 1951, and its colors remained on active duty until 1954. During its Korean service, the 231st became a fully integrated unit. The 936th Field Artillery Battalion from Fayetteville, Arkansas, was the first ARNG unit to enter combat in Korea. Armed with towed 155mm howitzers, the battalion entered active federal service on August 21, 1950, and after five months of stateside training arrived at Pusan on February 10, 1951. The 936th Field Artillery fired its first round against the communists on March 29 during an offensive to restore the front at the 38th Parallel. In one hundred days of heavy fire support, the Arkansas artillerymen fired a staggering 50,000 rounds, approximately one-third of the shells they had fired during 500 days of combat in World War II. The 40th and 45th Infantry Divisions were selected for service in Korea and, after extensive postmobilization training in the continental United States (CONUS) and Japan, entered combat in early 1952. (See figures 4-9 through 4-13.)

Guardsmen performed other important missions as well. An important task for the ARNG was to bolster NATO. Constabulary forces in Germany had been drained of personnel for Korea, and it fell to Guardsmen to deter against a feared Soviet attack in central

4-11 Oklahoma's 180th Infantry, an element of the 45th Infantry Division, saw hard fighting in Korea in early 1952. NARA

4-12 A forward observer of the 45th Infantry Division calls in an artillery mission in May 1952. NARA

Europe. The 28th and 43d Divisions went to Europe in April 1951 and took up defensive positions in central and southern Germany. Lastly, the Army's strategic reserve in CONUS had been depleted, and mobilized ARNG units served as a strategic reserve while acting as training and replacement depots for individual professional soldiers, activated reservists, and draftees going to and from Korea. Four more infantry divisions were called out for duty in CONUS: the 31st (Alabama and Mississippi), the 37th (Ohio), the 44th (Illinois), and the 47th (Minnesota and North Dakota). The 31st Division remained on duty at Fort Jackson, South Carolina, while the 37th Division went to Fort Polk, Louisiana and the 47th Division trained at Camp Rucker in Alabama. (See figure 4-14.) In anticipation of possible service in

4-13 An M-48 tank of the Tank Company, 180th Infantry, 45th Infantry Division, stands guard on a ridge in Korea. NARA

Korea, the 44th Division deployed to California for postmobilization training.

Peace negotiations started in November 1951, though the war dragged on until the signing of an armistice in July 1953. By the end of the war, approximately one-third of the ARNG had answered the call

to arms. The Korean mobilization remains the National Guard's most significant achievement after World War II.

### New Cold War Missions

Based on the lessons of the Korean War, the ARNG began to change its priorities for training. While the

4-14 Members of Minnesota's 175th Field Artillery Battalion, 47th Infantry Division, train with gas masks while on active duty in 1951. NGEF

4-15 Soldiers of the 186th Infantry (OR), 41st Infantry Division, practice marksmanship during annual training in 1954. NGEF

4-16 A DUWK of the 109th Transportation Truck Battalion (MN) moves troops during annual training at Camp Ripley, MN, 1955. NGEF

4-17 For a Guard unit, the armory is "home." By the 1950s some of the Guard's armories, such as this one in Ishpeming, MI, were quite dated and needed replacing. NGEF

4-18 With a large infusion of federal money, new and larger armories were constructed for weekend drills. This armory in Kansas City was dedicated in 1956. NGEF

Guard had concentrated formerly on preparing individuals for war, it now focused on training entire units for combat operations. Federal monies were made available for new armory construction that supported unit training. (See figures 4-15 through 4-19.)

Not wanting to invite another ground war in Asia, the Eisenhower administration adopted a strategy of "massive retaliation," which relied on nuclear weapons to deter war. Massive retaliation had two important influences on the ARNG. The Army focused on tactical nuclear warfare and converted several divisions to a new "pentomic" design that included five battle groups. By October 1959, the ARNG had completed a massive reorganization of its twenty-seven

4-19 Prior to World War I, most states established camps to train their Guard units. By the 1950s some, like Camp Ripley, MN, were quite extensive and saw use by Regular Army units as well as the Guard. NGEF

divisions to the pentomic organization, and Guardsmen took part in open-air nuclear tests in Nevada.

Secondly, the Guard became involved in the missile defense of the American homeland. The ARNG had already participated in the air defense of key industrial sites after

World War II with heavy antiaircraft artillery units. (See figure 4-20.) In June 1957 California's 720th Missile Battalion was the first ARNG unit to man a domestic missile site in anticipation of an enemy air attack. The object of missile defenses was to shoot down

Soviet heavy bombers intent on attacking American cities and industrial centers with nuclear weapons. By 1961 eighty-two ARNG NIKE-AJAX batteries were operational at key defensive locations in fifteen different states. At the program's peak in 1962, 17,000 Guardsmen manned missile sites. As early as 1958, the Army began to replace NIKE-AJAX with the NIKE-HER-CULES, a missile of increased speed, range, ceiling, and payload. At the zenith of the NIKE-HER-CULES program, Guardsmen manned 48 of the 112 missile sites defending CONUS. The rise of the intercontinental ballistic missile as the major nuclear threat resulted in the cancellation of the NIKE-HERCULES program, and by September 1974 the ARNG had closed all of its missile sites. (See figures 4-21 and 4-22.)

An unexpected National Guard assignment in 1957 portended future national events. In Arkansas, Governor Orville Faubus called out the National Guard to prevent racial integration in the public schools. President Dwight D. Eisenhower outflanked the governor by ordering the entire Arkansas National Guard into active federal service. In all instances, Guardsmen obeyed the president's orders. The Arkansas school system was integrated, and the incident marked the beginning of nearly twenty years of social, political, and economic turmoil that engulfed American society.

4-20 Men of Battery A, 380th Anti-Aircraft Artillery Battalion (Washington, DC), dash to their 120mm guns during an alert, 1957. NGEF

4-21 NIKE-AJAX antiaircraft missiles ready to launch. VANG

4-22 In the early 1960s the more powerful and effective NIKE-HERCULES replaced the AJAX. NGEF

4-23 Soldiers of Texas's 49th Armored Division dismount from an armored personnel carrier while on active duty at Ft. Polk, LA, during the Berlin Crisis in 1961. TXMM

## The Berlin Crisis

President John F. Kennedy entered office in January 1961 and months later was put to the test when the Soviets began construction of a formidable wall that split Berlin. On July 25, Kennedy put the military on alert and sought to mobilize the National Guard. Within a week, Congress authorized the call-up of 250,000 Guardsmen and reservists for twelve months.

ARNG units were activated in the fall of 1961. In early October, 44,317 ARNG soldiers were ordered to active federal service. The 32d Infantry Division (Wisconsin), the 49th Armored Division (Texas), the 150th Armored Cavalry Regiment (West Virginia), and 264

nondivisional units reported for duty, though none went overseas. The Berlin Crisis was the first time the United States used a reserve component mobilization as a political instrument to deter war. The call-up of Guardsmen to defend NATO displayed America's resolve to friends and foes alike. The Soviets eventually backed down, and by the late summer of 1962, all Guardsmen returned home. (See figures 4-23, 4-24, and 4-25.)

Still, the Berlin Crisis mobilization uncovered a number of shortcomings. The ARNG required the infusion of nearly 10,000 Army Reservists to flesh out units. President Kennedy's secretary of defense, Robert S. McNamara, believed the entire

4-24 Officers of Texas's 49th Armored Division on a field exercise during the Berlin Crisis. NGEF

4-25 Vehicles of the 150th Armored Cavalry Regiment (WV) "hit the beach" at Ft. Miles, DE, during Exercise Wethorse II during the Berlin Crisis, 1962. NGEF

4-26 The 3d Squadron, 116th Armored Cavalry (ID), wearing traditional frontier cavalry uniforms, salutes President Lyndon B. Johnson during his 1965 inaugural. NGEF

Defense Department needed major reforms to increase efficiency. Guard reforms that had started in the 1950s continued during McNamara's tenure. To improve readiness and training, the ARNG began extended monthly drill periods on weekends instead of weeknight drills. By 1966 NGB mandated weekend training for the ARNG, and the phrase "weekend warrior" became a household expression. Secretary McNamara took several steps to improve Guard readiness and deployability. Increased defense spending allowed the issue of new items to replace World War II weapons and equipment, and Army Guardsmen began flying on new, Air Guard transports to overseas training locations. (See figures 4-26 through 4-29.)

## The Vietnam War

North Vietnamese communists commenced operations in 1960 to conquer South Vietnam. President Kennedy took a stand against communist expansion, and by 1963, 16,000 U.S. advisers were in South Vietnam. After Kennedy's assassination, President Lyndon B. Johnson reaffirmed American backing for South Vietnam. In August 1964 Congress gave Johnson wide authority to prosecute the war.

In 1965 the United States committed 20,000 combat troops to South Vietnam. Against the recommendations of his top advisers, the president refused to mobilize the nation's reserve components. Johnson had no desire to provoke a major conflict in Southeast Asia, and he believed that calling out the Guard and Reserves might escalate the war. In the end, Johnson fought the war with active forces and draftees. Denied the opportunity to serve in Vietnam, individual Guardsmen volunteered. Approximately 2,000 ARNG volunteers fought in Vietnam, half of them officers. They provided distinguished service, and twenty-three were killed.

4-27 Army Guard troops exit an Air Guard C-130 in the 1960s. NGEF

4-28 An M-113 of the 127th Infantry (WI) tears up Fort McCoy, WI, during annual training. NGEF

To aid the war effort, the Defense Department created the Selected Reserve Force (SRF), a 150,000-man composite force of ARNG and U.S. Army Reserve units. The SRF's mission was to act as a strategic hedge against threats in Korea, Europe, and elsewhere. The ARNG provided nearly 120,00 combat and combat support troops to the SRF in three composite infantry divisions, six separate brigades, and an armored cavalry regiment. (See figures 4-30 and 4-31.)

Events in 1968 finally prompted a partial Guard mobilization. On January 23 the North Koreans seized the USS *Pueblo*. Only eight days later, the North Vietnamese launched the Tet Offensive, a massive effort to defeat American and South Vietnamese forces. The Tet Offensive surprised American commanders, and additional troops were rushed to Vietnam.

4-29 Nebraska's 24th Medical Company received two experimental UH-19D medivac helicopters in 1968 for evacuating victims of automobile crashes to distant hospitals. NENG

On April 11 President Johnson ordered 24,500 National Guardsmen and reservists to active duty.

On May 13, 1968, nearly 14,000 Army Guardsmen reported to their armories. Two ARNG infantry brigades were called up: Hawaii's 29th and Kansas's 69th. Though the brigades never deployed, 4,000 Guardsmen from their ranks volunteered for Vietnam. Thirty-one combat support and combat service support units served on various Army posts for extended active duty. Eight ARNG units went to war. (See figures 4-32 and 4-33.) The 650th Medical Detachment (Alabama) was the first unit to reach Vietnam. The only ARNG ground maneuver unit sent to Vietnam was Com-

pany D (Ranger), 151st Infantry, from Indiana. (See figure 4-34.) On December 12, 1969, the last mobilized Army Guardsman returned home; more than 9,000 ARNG soldiers served in Vietnam.

## America Burns, 1965–1970

While the fighting in Vietnam raged, the National Guard quelled antiwar and race riots throughout America. The first major civil disturbance of the 1960s started in Watts, Los Angeles, on August 11, 1965, when a confrontation between police officers and black youths sparked widespread rioting. The following day, California's governor called out the Guard. Soldiers occupied roadblocks, confronted angry crowds and provided protection to firefighters. Over the following week, rioting killed 35 people and injured 1,000. By the time it ended, 13,393 Guardsmen had seen duty. (See figure 4-35.)

Rioting in Detroit required the involvement of Regular and National Guard troops. A police raid on a black nightclub on July 23, 1967,

**4-30 Members of Kansas's 69th Infantry Brigade, part of the Selected Reserve Force in 1966, practice their marksmanship skills. NGEF**

**4-31 Guardsmen on the mortar range, 1970. NGEF**

**4-32 Cannoneers of the 3d Battalion, 197th Field Artillery (NH), load a 155mm howitzer to support allied forces near Phu Loi, Vietnam, 1969. NGEF**

sparked widespread rioting. By the next day, 8,000 Guardsmen were in Detroit, but looting, arson, and vandalism intensified. Finally, President Johnson ordered 5,000 active-duty soldiers to Detroit. The over-whelming show of force restored order by the end of the month, but the final tally was shocking: 42 dead and 1,000 injured, including some Guardsmen. (See figure 4-36.)

During 1968, 105,000 Guardsmen participated in riot-control duty. The worst civil disturbances occurred in April in the aftermath of the assassination of Dr. Martin Luther King Jr. To control riots in Detroit, Washington, D.C., Chicago, and Baltimore, 25,000 Guardsmen were ordered to active duty. During 1969 and 1970 race riots and antiwar demonstrations

4-33 Idaho's 116th Engineer Battalion (Combat) at Bao Loc, Vietnam, 1969. NGEF

continued, but their frequency and intensity waned. (See figure 4-37.)

One of the most unfortunate moments in National Guard history came in May 1970. A fierce, antiwar riot broke out at Kent State University in north-eastern Ohio on May 2, and students burned the ROTC building. The following day, Ohio

Guardsmen converged on the campus. On May 4, 2,500 stu-dents gathered to chant antiwar slogans and to hurl rocks and obscenities at the Guardsmen. Civil authorities ordered more than 100 armed Guardsmen to clear the campus, but the pro-testers hurled rocks, bricks, and bottles causing dozens of inju-ries. Afraid for their lives and

4-34 Members of Indiana's Company D (Long Range Patrol), 151st Infantry, move out of their base at "Camp Atterbury East" near Saigon, Vietnam, January 18, 1969. NGEF

4-35 Guardsmen of the 40th Armored Division direct traffic away from the riot-torn area of Watts, Los Angeles, in 1965. NGEF

angered by the students' actions, thirty Guardsmen unleashed a volley of rifle fire that killed four protesters and wounded nine others. (See figures 4-38 and 4-39.)

## The All-Volunteer Force

The end of the draft came as a direct result of the nation's bitter experience in Vietnam. After assuming office in 1969, President Richard M. Nixon promised to end the draft. Realizing that an all-volunteer force was inevitable, the armed forces launched programs to ease the transition to volunteerism. The military increased its recruiting force, initiated family and bachelor housing, and raised education benefits. After a near-continuous stint since 1940, the draft ended on July 1, 1973.

Because of the end of both the Vietnam War and the draft, the ARNG experienced a severe personnel crisis. The National Guard enacted new recruiting programs and developed a dedicated recruiting force to maintain its strength. In 1977 alone, 104,000 Vietnam-era volunteers fled the ARNG. By the end of the 1970s, ARNG strength bottomed out at 346,974 soldiers, a 20 percent decline from the close of the Vietnam War. Increased minority participation allowed the ARNG to endure the personnel crisis. In 1971, only 4,961 African American soldiers were in the Army Guard. As a result of an intense recruiting

4-36 Michigan Guardsmen of the 46th Infantry Division protect a fire truck during the Detroit riot in 1967. NGEF

4-37 Soldiers of the 487th Field Artillery Battalion (HI) practice riot control techniques at Schofield Barracks, March 1968. NGEF

4-38 Ohio Guardsmen deployed on the campus of Kent State University, May 1970. KENT

4-39 The 163d Military Police Battalion (Washington, D.C.) confronts antiwar protesters during the May 1970 anti-Vietnam rally in Washington, D.C. During this disturbance the NGAUS Memorial was damaged by a bomb. DCNG

4-41 SP4 Louis Hudson of the 190th Military Police Company (GA) was one of the many African Americans joining the Guard in the 1970s. NGEF

4-40 With racial integration in the 1960s, African Americans played an increasingly important role in the Guard's overall strength. NGEF

4-42 First Lt. Sylvia Marie St. Charles Law, a member of Alabama's 109th Evacuation Hospital in 1957, was the first woman to join the Army Guard. NGEF

effort, black participation in the ARNG skyrocketed. (See figures 4-40 and 4-41.) Five years later, 46,696 African Americans made up more than 12 percent of the ARNG. Female participation in the National Guard as nurse officers had started in the 1950s, but women joined the ranks in increasing numbers after Vietnam. In 1972 only fifty-six officer and enlisted women were in the ARNG, but five years later, more than 11,000 females were on duty. (See figures 4-42 through 4-45.)

4-43 In the summer of 1957, Guardswomen, such as these members of California's 143d Evacuation Hospital, first attended annual training. **NGEF**

4-45 Many of the job specialties women perform require highly technical skills. This member of Nebraska's 24th Medical Company (Air Ambulance) is shown doing helicopter maintenance. **NENG**

## The Total Force Policy

The Total Force Policy allowed the National Guard to weather the austere budget and personnel environment of the 1970s. In August 1973 Defense Secretary James R. Schlesinger announced that the services were to fully integrate their active and reserve forces into a "homogeneous whole." Without the draft, the Guard and Reserves were to be the initial, primary, and sole augmentation to active forces.

The Total Force Policy drew the ARNG and the active Army into closer harmony. In an effort to strengthen the Army and avoid another unpopular war, Army Chief of Staff General Creighton W. Abrams Jr., initiated the Roundout Program. ARNG Roundout Brigades formed the third combat brigades of

4-44 As the Guard attempted to keep its strength up after the end of the draft, women became a ready source of new recruits. **NGEF**

4-46 Two native members of the Alaska Scout Battalion train with Canadian soldiers in 1962. NGEF

4-48 In 1975, marking the bicentennial of the American Revolution, members of the 152d Infantry (MI), 38th Infantry Division, march in a parade, wearing historic uniforms from the Revolutionary and Civil Wars, plus World Wars I and II. NGEF

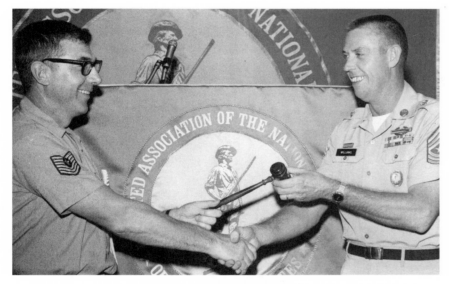

4-47 The presidency of the Enlisted Association of the National Guard passes from Army to Air in the 1970s. The Association supported the Total Force Policy of the period. NGEF

designated Regular Army divisions and, in General Abrams's mind, formed a vital link between the American people and the Army. At the same time, more Guardsmen deployed overseas for periodic training. Army Guardsmen trained with other nations' reserve components and traveled to Europe for annual deployments. By 1980, 6,500 ARNG soldiers had traveled overseas for training. (See figures 4-46 through 4-53.)

American weakness in the 1970s prompted Soviet ventures around the world. Communists made gains in Latin America,

4-49 During the 1970s, the Guard received AH-1D "Cobra" attack helicopters. NGEF

4-50 A Guard CH-47 "Chinook" helicopter has just delivered men of California's 670th Military Police Company in 1974. NGEF

4-51 Members of Wichita's 242d Engineer Company (KS) conduct preventive maintenance on their vehicles before leaving for annual training, 1970. NGEF

4-52 Members of Hawaii's 299th Infantry, 29th Infantry Brigade, play "aggressors" during an exercise. NGEF

4-53 Basic training up through the 1970s included "doing the bars" to increase upper arm strength. NGEF

4-54 Soldiers of Company B, 121st Engineer Battalion (MD), construct a "Bailey Bridge" in 1983. MDNG

Africa, and the Middle East. In 1979 Islamic fundamentalists in Iran seized nearly 200 American hostages, and the Soviets invaded Afghanistan. The 1980s would witness a resurgent America under the leadership of a new president.

## The Reagan Buildup

President Ronald W. Reagan entered office in January 1981 promising to restore national power and prestige. Concerned over communist advances around the world, Reagan was determined to square off against the Soviet Union. The instrument for confronting communism would be a revitalized U.S. military.

The Reagan Buildup began at a time when the armed forces had deteriorated badly. With greatly increased budgets, the Army recovered from the damage of the Vietnam War and the neglect of the 1970s. Funding went toward new, high-technology weapons ranging from tanks to attack helicopters. Regulars and Guardsmen went through tough, realistic exercises at the Army's new, premier training site, the National Training Center (NTC), at Fort Irwin, California. (See figures 4-54, 4-55, and 4-56.)

The most important gains in the ARNG came in manpower that grew steadily throughout the 1980s. Increased recruiting budgets, flexible enlistment options, educational incentives, and a professional recruiting force promoted volunteerism. By 1989 ARNG personnel strength reached a historic peacetime

4-55 Flying drones, known as "radio controlled aerial targets" (RCATs), were used for air defense artillery practice. Members of the 200th Air Defense Artillery Detachment (NM) prepare an RCAT for flight in the 1980s. NGEF

4-56 Mississippi Guardsmen race to board a UH-60A "Blackhawk" helicopter in 1985. NGEF

high of 456,960 soldiers. Minorities made up nearly one-quarter of the ARNG. By 1989, 75,000 African-American Guardsmen comprised more than 16 percent of the force. At the same time, nearly 30,000 female soldiers constituted over 6 percent of the ARNG. (See figure 4-57.)

With the growth in manpower came an increase in units. The 35th Infantry Division (Mechanized) was activated in 1984, and a year later the 29th Infantry Division (Light) was

4-57 Though barred by law from direct combat positions, women served in combat support roles by the 1980. Members of the Support Battalion, 116th Infantry Brigade (VA), prepare for training. VANG

## Congressman G. V. "Sonny" Montgomery: National Guard Soldier and Statesman

Congressman G. V. "Sonny" Montgomery stands as one of the National Guard's most important advocates in the second half of the twentieth century. During World War II, he served as a lieutenant in the 12th Armored Division in Europe. After the war, he returned home to Mississippi and joined the National Guard. Montgomery was mobilized with the 31st Infantry Division for the Korean War and remained on active duty until 1952.

After the Korean War, Sonny Montgomery was elected to the Mississippi legislature and served there for ten years. He had his first national exposure in 1962 while commanding a detachment of Mississippi Guardsmen ordered to safeguard Dr. Martin Luther King Jr.'s Freedom Ride to Jackson, Mississippi. He returned from the Mississippi Guard with the state rank of major general.

In 1966 Sonny Montgomery was elected to the U.S. House of representatives, where he became a principal advocate for personnel in the all-volunteer military. In the early 1980s he sponsored a new Montgomery G.I. Bill that gave service members important enlistment and education benefits. Tens of thousands of Guardsmen and women eventually took advantage of the program. In 1987 Congress formalized the Montgomery G.I. Bill. The same year he sponsored the Montgomery Amendment, a key piece of legislation that supported overseas training for Guardsmen and paved the way for the U.S. Supreme Court's 1990 Perpich decision. During the Persian Gulf War, Congressman Montgomery was a key supporter for the mobilization and deployment of ARNG combat units.

Sonny Montgomery retired from Congress in 1996 after thirty years of distinguished service. The impressive Montgomery Room in the national Guard Memorial in Washington, D.C., is a fitting tribute to this outstanding soldier-statesman. Because of this long-term advocacy for National Guard issues, Sonny Montgomery stands as one of the most important Guard legislators since World War II.

**4-58 The 29th Infantry Division (Light) was reactivated in October 1985. VANG**

reformed. (See figure 4-58.) Increases in the Roundout Program also occurred. Mississippi's 155th Armored Brigade became a Roundout to the 1st Cavalry Division at Fort Hood, Texas, and New York's 27th Infantry Brigade rounded out the new 10th Mountain Division at Fort Drum, New York. In 1990 the 116th Cavalry Brigade, with units in Idaho, Oregon, and Nevada, became the last ARNG brigade to achieve Roundout status.

Overseas deployments became the foundation of ARNG training. The Guard's participation in the Army's annual deployment of

4-60 Maj. Gen. G. V. "Sonny" Montgomery

4-62 Corpsmen of the 135th Medical Company (WI) treat a casualty while dressed in full chemical protective gear, 1985. NGEF

4-61 Army Guard engineers constructing a bridge in Central America in the 1980s. NGB

forces to West Germany increased each year. The greatest participation in such exercises occurred in 1986 when the 32d Infantry Brigade from Wisconsin deployed to West Germany with all of its equipment and personnel. In 1985 the first Guardsmen went to the Middle East on Bright Star exercises, and in the Pacific, Guardsmen deployed to Korea on Team Spirit. ARNG soldiers experienced the best training during tough, realistic maneuvers at the NTC. (See figure 4-60.)

Beginning in 1983 the National Guard participated in extensive training missions in Central America. A road-building program—Fuertes Caminos (Blazing Trails)—became the centerpiece of the Guard's efforts. (See figures 4-61 and 4-62.) Several governors opposed to the Reagan administration's foreign policy objected outright to the ARNG's use in Central America. A three-year court battle ensued over the rights of the governors to deny their consent to overseas training. In the June 1990 Perpich decision, the U.S. Supreme Court declared that the authority of the states to train the militia did not limit the president's authority to train Guard personnel on active duty as reserves of the Army. (See figure 4-63.)

## The Persian Gulf War

On August 2, 1990, Iraq launched a sudden invasion of the small, oil-rich emirate of Kuwait at the head of the Persian Gulf. By occupying Kuwait, Iraq's Saddam Hussein hoped to increase his stature as an Arab leader and his control over the world's oil supplies. Within days, a UN coalition headed by President George Bush retaliated against Iraq. Allied war aims were clear: Saddam Hussein was to withdraw from Kuwait and allow the full restoration of the Kuwaiti government.

On August 6, President Bush announced Operation Desert Shield, the buildup of Allied forces in the Gulf. Two weeks later, the president ordered Guardsmen and reservists to active duty in the largest mobilization since the Korean War. Between August 1990 and the end of Operation Desert Storm on February 28, 1991, a total of 74,815 National Guard soldiers and airmen entered active duty. (See figure 4-64.)

The first ARNG units entered active duty on August 27. Before the crisis ended, 62,411 Army Guardsmen in 398 units had served. Soldiers from forty-eight states, the District of Columbia, Guam, and Puerto Rico were ordered to active duty in thirty-six increments. All of the Guardsmen called reported for duty. In the early stages of Desert Shield, 129 units mobilized between August 27 and November 17. As the prospects for war increased, the buildup accelerated. The largest increment occurred on November 21, when sixty units were mobilized. Between November 21 and the opening of Operation Desert Storm on January 17, 1991, another 233 units were federalized.

The first ARNG unit arrived in Saudi Arabia on September 9, and nearly 300 ARNG units

4-62 Medics of the 405th Combat Support Hospital (CT) treat villagers in Xococ, Guatemala, 1992. NGEF

4-63 PFC Charla Shull receives the Panama Service Ribbon from Missouri Governor John Ashcroft after returning with her unit, the 1138th Military Police Company from Panama in 1989. She was the first Guardswoman to come under direct enemy fire when her unit was mortared during Operation Just Cause. She served in the Gulf War with the same unit. NGB

4-64 Members of the 249th Engineer Detachment (DE) go through mobilization processing before deploying to Saudi Arabia. NGEF

4-65 Maryland Guardsmen arrive in Saudi Arabia during Desert Shield, 1990. NGB

eventually served in Southwest Asia. (See figure 4-65.) Guardsmen dispersed across the desert to perform missions as diverse as logistics, transportation, traffic control, water purification, and military police. When Desert Storm began on January 17, approximately 23,000 ARNG soldiers were already on hand. When the war ended six weeks later, more than 37,000 Army Guardsmen were in country. Two field artillery brigades—the 142d from Arkansas and Oklahoma and the 196th from Tennessee, Kentucky, and West Virginia—were the only ARNG combat troops to see action. A balanced force of thirty battalions ranging from field artillery to quartermaster provided a diverse range of combat, combat support, and combat service support capabilities. (See figures 4-66 through 4-69.)

4-66 Guardsmen of the 212th Engineer Company (TN) stay warm against the early morning chill along the Iraqi–Saudi border just after the start of Desert Storm, January 1991. They constructed supply roads for coalition forces. NGEF

4-67 A team from the 103d Public Affairs Detachment (MT) raises their flag inside Iraq thirty minutes after the cease-fire, February 28, 1991. NGEF

4-68 Displaying the same unit and state pride as their predecessors in the 937th Field Artillery in the Korean War, Arkansas Guardsmen of the 142d Field Artillery (the 937th descendant unit) carry on the tradition during Desert Storm, January 1991. NGEF

4-69 Military policemen of Michigan's 1776th MP Company construct a prisoner of war compound on the Iraqi–Kuwait border in February 1991. NGEF

More than one hundred ARNG units remained in the United States or deployed to Europe to replace active forces rushing to the Gulf. Sixteen ARNG units went to Europe for a variety of support missions. Eighty-five units remained stateside on active-duty posts, performing duties normally done by Regulars.

Nearly 13,000 Army Guardsmen ordered to active duty were assigned to the 48th Infantry (Georgia), 256th Infantry (Louisiana), and 155th Armored (Mississippi) Brigades, Roundout units to active Army divisions. For three months, the brigades waited for the call that finally came on November 8. As war loomed, the Roundout brigades comprised a ready, national reserve against the possibility of a protracted campaign in the Persian Gulf or a regional crisis elsewhere.

The 48th Brigade entered active duty on November 30 and

moved immediately to Fort Stewart, Georgia. After an initial training period, troops and equipment deployed to the NTC at Fort Irwin for additional exercises. On February 28, ninety-one days after mobilization and the same day that Desert Storm ended, Army leaders certified the 48th Brigade as combat ready.

By December 7, the 256th, and 155th Brigades had been ordered to active duty. The 256th Brigade reported to Fort Polk, Louisiana, while the 155th Brigade went to Fort Hood, Texas. By late January, the two brigades were concentrated at Fort Hood for large-scale maneuvers. After Desert Storm ended, all three brigades returned to their mobilization stations and were released from active duty by May 14. (See figures 4-70 and 4-71.)

## Downsizing and Domestic Duty

With the fall of the Berlin Wall in 1989, plans for reducing U.S. military forces were developed even before the start of the Gulf War. President Bush advocated cuts of up to one-quarter of the entire military, a precedent that endured and intensified during the administration of President William J. Clinton.

Starting in 1992, the ARNG endured a painful series of unit and personnel cuts. The Army Guard shrank from an all-time high of 457,000 soldiers in 1989 down to 357,400 personnel ten years later. The Guard lost the

4-70 Oklahoma's 745th Military Police Company returned home from the Gulf War in May 1991. NGEF

4-71 The 3d Battalion, 141st Infantry (TX), was assigned to Mississippi's 155th Armored Brigade during preparations for possible deployment during Desert Storm. NGEF

4-72 During the 1990s, a number of Guard artillery units converted to the multiple launch rocket system (MLRS). NGEF

4-73 Equipment upgrades in the 1990s included AH-64 "Apache" attack helicopters. NGEF

4-74 An M-1 "Abrams" tank crew of Idaho's 116th Cavalry Brigade takes a break at the National Training Center at Fort Irwin, CA. NGEF

equivalent of two divisions and eleven combat brigades. In 1993 the Off-Site Agreement, a long-range plan that realigned the Army along functional lines, made the ARNG primarily responsible for reserve combat units. The Army decided that instead of eliminating much-needed field artillery battalions, those units belonged in the Guard. Eventually, the ARNG contained 70 percent of all the Army's artillery. (See figures 4-72, 4-73, and 4-74.)

Even as the ARNG shrank, it played an important role in providing emergency assistance during large domestic emergencies. In April 1992 the Rodney King riot exploded in south-central Los Angeles and developed into the most violent and widespread urban rioting since the late 1960s. More than 10,000 California Guardsmen helped to restore order. Guard units included a cross-section of minority soldiers that reflected the racial diversity of southern California, a factor that many believed increased the Guard's effectiveness in dealing with rioters. In August 1992 Hurricane Andrew tore across the southern tip of Florida, causing the most extensive property damage of any storm in U.S. history. Eventually, 6,000 Guardsmen participated in the recovery effort. The following year, the most severe flooding in 500 years occurred along the upper Mississippi River. During

4-75 Soldiers of the 49th Military Police Brigade (CA) assisted the Los Angeles fire department during the Rodney King riot in 1992. NGEF

4-76 Natural disasters know no boundaries. Two Alabama Quartermaster companies specializing in water purification aided an Iowa hospital when the Mississippi River flooded Des Moines. NGEF

4-77 When the Mississippi River flooded much of the Midwest in 1993, thousands of Army Guardsmen were called to state active duty to erect flood barricades. NGEF

4-78 In the wake of Hurricane Andrew in August 1992, units of the Florida Guard were called in to support relief efforts. Vehicles of the 2d Battalion, 124th Infantry, on alert at the Culter Ridge Police station. NGEF

the summer of 1993, nearly 8,400 Guardsmen brought aid to flood ravaged towns. In addition, Guard soldiers assisted in the recovery from various hurricanes that affected Hawaii and Guam. (See figures 4-75 through 4-79.)

Despite the end of the Cold War, the ARNG continued to hone its fighting skills with tough training and realistic exercises. Soldiers in combat, combat support, and combat service support units learned and

improved abilities that made them more effective during federal and state missions. ARNG soldiers gained new high-technology skills when units received administrative and tactical computers. (See figure

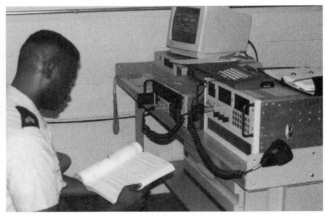

4-80 Starting in the 1960s and continuing through to the present day, the Guard has sought to acquire the latest in computer equipment. **NGB**

4-79 Helping to repair the damage of Supertyphoon "Paka," the 1224th Engineer Detachment, Guam National Guard, removes debris in 1994. **NGEF**

4-81 SSG James Solomon from the Hawaii Guard trains in the cold rain of Fort Lewis, WA, in 1984. **NGEF**

4-82 Soldiers of the 115th Infantry (MD), 29th Infantry Division (Light), experience the realistic feel of city combat at the Combat Maneuver Training Center at Hohenfels, Germany, in January 1996. **NGEF**

4-83 An M2-A2 "Bradley" from Troop E, 303d Cavalry (WA), fires an antitank missile while training at the Yakima Training Center, 1996. NGB

4-84 Guardsmen from Alaska's Long-Range Surveillance Detachment rappel from an UH-1H helicopter in 1996. NGB

4-80.) From the M-1 tank to the microprocessor, Guard soldiers mastered the techniques of modern warfare. (See figures 4-81 through 4-87).

## Guardsmen as Peacekeepers

With the end of the Cold War, the strategy of containing communism gave way to peacetime engagement. Through its involvement in regional crises, the United States hoped to prevent political, ethnic, and racial hatreds from escalating into larger wars. ARNG soldiers first became involved in peacekeeping operations in 1994 when individuals with special training and technical skills deployed to Somalia to assist in the withdrawal of U.S. forces from the Horn of Africa. In 1995 ARNG Special Forces and aviation units served in Haiti as part of a larger American peacekeeping effort. (See figure 4-88.) That

4-85 Members of Rhode Island's 19th Special Forces Group receive water training in Hawaii, 1997. NGEF

4-86 Sgt. Michael Bouger from Vermont listens to range commands during a National Guard marksmanship competition. **NGB**

4-87 SPC Charles Johnston is a sniper in the 299th Infantry (HI), 29th Infantry Brigade (Separate), 1995. **NGB**

same year, a composite battalion of Regular, Guard, and Army Reserve troops deployed to the Sinai Desert as part of a long-term peacekeeping commitment to guarantee peace between Israel and Egypt.

The ARNG's greatest contributions as a peacekeeping force occurred in the Balkans. After years of brutal warfare, the states of the former Yugoslavia negotiated a peace in late 1995 that required the presence of NATO peacekeepers. During the 1996–99 period, the ARNG deployed nearly 10,000 peacekeepers to the former Yugoslavia and Macedonia. In late 1997 Company C, 3-116th Infantry, from Virginia deployed to Bosnia, becoming the first ARNG ground maneuver unit to go in harms' way since the Vietnam War. In 2000 the headquarters of the 49th Armored Division from Texas became the controlling headquarters for U.S. peacekeeping operations, the first time an ARNG division headquarters had deployed to NATO since the Korean War. And the presence of ARNG peacekeepers in the Balkans seems assured as long as the United States remains engaged there. (See figures 4-89 through 4-92.)

## The War on Terror

On September 11, 2001, America suffered its greatest surprise attack in history with the horrific terrorist assaults on the Pentagon in Washington, D.C., and the World Trade Center in New York City. At the Pentagon, Guard

4-88 Soldiers of the 20th Special Forces Group (AL) train prior to deployment to Haiti in 1995. NGEF

4-89 A West Virginia unit uses a United Nations M-113 to transport supplies to civilians in war-ravaged Sarajevo, Bosnia. NGEF

4-90 One of the first Army Guard units to deploy to Bosnia was the 161st Target Acquisition Detachment (KS), 35th Infantry Division. Members are working with French soldiers of Operation Joint Endeavor, 1996. KSNG

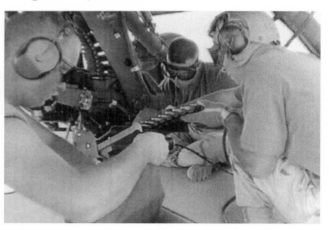

4-91 Guard members of Task Force Panther in Kuwait load ammunition into an AH-64 attack helicopter during Operation Desert Fox, 1999. NGB

medical personnel helped to rescue and treat survivors. In New York City, ARNG soldiers rushed to the scene of the crisis in lower Manhattan. Citizen-soldiers manned a security perimeter around the World Trade Center debris field, as-sisted in the recovery effort, and gave aid and comfort to the survivors and the friends and families of the missing. (See figures 4-93 and 4-94.)

Since September 11, the

4-92 ARNG peacekeepers on patrol in Bosnia in late 1997. KACMARCIK

4-94 ARNG soldiers volunteered to work alongside New York City policemen and firefighters in the bucket lines used to excavate debris from the World Trade Center. NGB

4-93 Soldiers of New York's 105th Infantry man a security barricade surrounding the World Trade Center debris field. Expressions of thanks and support from school children across the nation are displayed on the barricade. NGB

4-95 Military policemen from the Virginia Guard patrol Ronald Reagan National Airport in Washington, D.C., when it reopened following the September 11 attacks. NGB

4-96 Sgt. Sean Selden of Michigan's 1775th Military Police Company answers a radio call while assisting customs agents on the United States–Canadian border at Port Huron, Michigan. NGB

ARNG has been a key participant in Operation Noble Eagle, the homeland defense portion of the war on terrorism. On any given day, as many as 25,000 Guard soldiers are on duty across the nation. Immediately following the initial terrorist attacks, more than 9,000 citizen soldiers helped to improve security at 422 commercial airports across the country. (See figure 4-95). Guardsmen inspected more than one hundred suspicious letters and packages thought to have contained chemical substances or explosives. Army Guard troops augmented customs agents at the busiest crossing sites on the Canadian and Mexican borders and increased security at a number of ports of entry. (See figure 4-96.) In the nation's capital, members of the District of Columbia National Guard helped the Capitol Police to provide security at the Capitol Hill complex. (See figure 4-97). Guard men and women have served on extensive security details at the World Series, the New York City Marathon, and the 2002 Winter Olympic Games. (See figure 4-98). In each instance, they helped to provide a safe and secure venue for these popular, public events.

The National Guard has acted not only as a homeland

4-98 Members of the Utah ARNG provide security at the Salt Lake City airport during the 2002 Winter Olympics. NGB

4-99 ARNG SF operators from the 20th SF Group based at Bagram Air Base north of Kabul, Afghanistan, prepare for a mission against Taliban and al Qaeda fighters. **NGB**

4-100 An Army CH-47 Chinook resupplies ARNG troops operating in the high deserts and mountains of Afghanistan. **NGB**

security force but has proved itself as a full-fledged combat reserve during the war on terrorism's overseas campaigns. The September 11 attacks demanded a military response, and the object of America's wrath became Osama bin Laden's al Qaeda terrorist network based in Afghanistan. The Taliban, a Muslim fundamentalist government bent on establishing a strict Islamic theocracy, had seized power in Afghanistan years earlier, allowing al Qaeda to establish training camps there while planning and plotting terrorist attacks worldwide.

On October 7, 2001, the United States and other allied nations launched an invasion of Afghanistan, code-named Operation Enduring Freedom (OEF). The campaign's objectives were to destroy al Qaeda and remove the Taliban. What followed was a rapid campaign of high-technology and precision aerial firepower, mixed with

Special Forces (SF) operators and indigenous fighters on the ground, which toppled the Taliban in a matter of weeks. However, al Qaeda fighters eluded coalition forces by seeking refuge in the high mountains of eastern Afghanistan. Through the winter and spring of 2001–2002, the troops saw hard fighting as U.S. and coalition forces battled a stubborn enemy amid the cold, snowy mountaintops.

The ARNG provided a small number of highly specialized personnel for OEF's first phase. The war placed a premium on intelligence specialists and Arabic linguists. These specially trained citizen-soldiers saw extensive service during the war, often performing unique missions in dangerous places. However, the ARNG's greatest contribution early in OEF came with the deployment of the 19th and 20th SF Groups. By February 2002, hundreds of ARNG SF

operators were on the ground in Afghanistan to assist active-duty SF units in the hunt for bin Laden. Guard SF members also searched former al Qaeda training camps for valuable intelligence and combed the Afghan mountains for enemy hideouts and weapons caches. (See figures 4-99 and 4-100.)

In late 2003, the ARNG assumed the primary responsibility for Task Force Phoenix, a coalition program designed to train the new Afghan National Army. Oklahoma's 45th Enhanced Brigade was the first ARNG command to assume the mission. When the Guardsmen arrived near Kabul, only a few hundred trained soldiers were in the new army's ranks, but over the following months, the Oklahomans trained almost 14,000 troops. In 2004, Indiana's 76th Brigade assumed command of Task Force Phoenix, and other brigades have continued the training program. The long-term plan is to train 70,000 soldiers for

4-101 An instructor from Florida's 53rd Infantry Brigade begins a training session with members of the new Afghan National Army at the Kabul Military Training Center. NGB

4-102 Capt. Scott Cadieux and other instructors from Vermont's 124th Regional Training Institute lead Afghan noncommissioned officers in a terrain board exercise at the Kabul Military Training Center. NGEF

the Afghan National Army by 2009. When the establishment of the Afghan National Army is complete, the ARNG will have helped transform the former sanctuary of Taliban and al Qaeda forces into an example for peace and freedom throughout the region. (See figures 4-101 and 102.)

In March 2003, the United States and other coalition forces opened another major front in the war on terrorism and by launching an invasion of Iraq. The main objective of Operation Iraqi Freedom (OIF) was to replace dictator Saddam Hussein's rogue regime with a democratic form of government that represented the Iraqi people. Coalition forces captured Baghdad in matter of weeks and ousted Saddam's regime; however, a determined insurgency of terrorists, guerrillas, and diehard Saddam loyalists soon rose up against the perceived coalition occupation.

4-103 A citizen-soldier from California's 1-184th Infantry shares candy with Iraqi children while on patrol. Establishing positive relations with local civilians helped to build trust between Iraqi civilians and ARNG soldiers. NGB

4-104 First Lt. Richard C. Smith, leading a night patrol near Forward Operation Base "Rough Rider" in Diyala Province, Iraq, questions local villagers concerning insurgent activities in the area. His unit Company B, 1st Battalion, 120th Infantry, 30th Infantry Brigade, from North Carolina, served in Iraq from February 2004 to January 2005. The man wearing the mask is his interpreter. NGB

4-105 The ARNG contains the majority of the Army's artillery battalions. A gun crew from Arkansas's 39th Infantry Brigade fires its artillery piece in support of coalition operations in Iraq. NGB

4-106 Small acts of humanity reduce the sting of war. Sergeant Littlewood of the Nebraska ARNG's 267th Ordnance Company provides comfort to an Iraqi mother and her children amid the chaos and danger of Iraq. NGB

4-107 Like their ancestors in World Wars I and II, members of New York's 42nd Infantry Division once again head to war. Division troops climb a jetway and enter a civilian, chartered airliner for the long flight to Iraq. NGB

The U.S. Army soon found itself battling an insurgency that took root within the cities of north and central Iraq. Strapped for manpower, the Army increasingly turned to citizen-soldiers to bear the unexpected burden. By the summer of 2005, the ARNG had provided half of the combat brigades fighting on the ground in Iraq. Citizen-soldiers from eight brigades participated in a full spectrum of activities, from providing humanitarian support and reconstruction to active patrols and outright combat operations against insurgents. Not since World War II had the nation relied so heavily on National Guard combat units, and the Army's senior leadership acknowledged the Army could not sustain its presence in Iraq without the ARNG. (See figures 4-103 through 4-106.)

One of the ARNG's greatest contributions to OIF occurred in February 2005 when New York's 42nd Infantry Division deployed to Iraq. The division assumed responsibility for a key sector in northern and central Iraq known as the "Sunni Triangle," which contained such trouble spots as Kirkuk and Tikrit. The 42nd Division headquarters controlled the operations of two ARNG and two active-duty combat brigades, a force of over 22,000 soldiers. For the first time since the Korean War, a National Guard combat division served in an active theater of war.

Guard soldiers helped to prepare, train, mentor, and fight alongside Iraqi Army forces battling insurgents. They also conducted stability operations designed to defeat insurgents and to destroy caches of weapons and ammunition. (See figure 4-107.)

Throughout its long history, members of the National Guard have often distinguished themselves for valor. In the war on terrorism, Sgt. Leigh Ann Hester holds top billing. Hester is the first female soldier since World War II to receive the nation's third-highest medal for valor, the Silver Star, and the first woman ever to receive the

4-108 Sgt. Leigh Ann Hester was featured on the cover of *Army* magazine in October 2005. AUSA

award for close combat. Hester deployed to Iraq with her Kentucky ARNG unit in November 2004. The 617th Military Police Company of Richmond, Kentucky, came under fire on March 20, 2005, when insurgents ambushed a thirty-truck convoy they were escorting twelve miles south of Baghdad.

Under St. Sgt. Timothy Nein's leadership, the MP squad drove its three Humvees into the line of fire to protect the convoy. Pinned in the middle of the kill zone by about fifty insurgents with AK-47s, machine guns, and rocket-propelled grenades, Nein leaped into the line of fire. From the Humvee behind him, Hester followed his lead and fired on insurgents wherever possible. She hit two immediately. Soon, insurgents surrounded the squad. Hester and Nein met them head-on with small arms fire, hand grenades, and aggressive maneuvering. The pair continued to charge forward under the cover of supporting fire, lobbing grenades and firing their assault rifles until the shooting stopped; the trenches and surrounding orchard were littered with bodies. The ARNG soldiers are believed to have killed twenty-seven insurgents. Sergeant Hester killed at least three and wounded many others. Hester, Nein, and Spc. Jason Mike of Radcliff, Kentucky, received the Silver Star for valor. (See figure 4-108.)

While the ARNG has distinguished itself during operations in Afghanistan and Iraq, that service has come at a price. As of July 2006, more than 400 Guard members have died during the war on terrorism, and the list of killed and wounded is expected to grow until the hostilities end.

Even as Guard troops served extensively in OEF and OIF, their mission as a domestic defense force remained as crucial as ever. One of the National Guard's most challenging domestic missions came with the rescue and recovery effort following Hurricane Katrina. The storm struck the Gulf Coast in the early morning hours of August 29, 2005, with howling winds, torrential rains, and an overwhelming tidal surge that resulted in one of the greatest natural disasters in American history. The following day, the storm's tidal surge breeched the levee system protecting New Orleans, and gushing floodwaters left much of the city in ruins. With all essential services disrupted and

4-109 In the immediate aftermath of Hurricane Katrina, federal and military agencies performed house-to-house searches to rescue citizens stranded by the floodwaters. A combined team of Drug Enforcement Agency officers and National Guard troops patrol a flooded New Orleans ward by truck searching for survivors and looters. NGB

4-110 Veterans of hurricane responses, Florida Guard units rushed to the Gulf Coast to add their expertise and support during Hurricane Katrina. Members of the Florida Guard load one of their Black Hawks with water and rations at the height of the humanitarian crisis. NGB

lawlessness gripping the city, local first responders faced the almost impossible tasks of removing the sick and the elderly and of evacuating the thousands left marooned. Not since the American Civil War has a major U.S. city been abandoned so completely. Hurricane Katrina left nearly 1,800 dead in the Gulf Coast states and was the most expensive natural disaster in American history.

The response to Hurricane Katrina resulted in the National Guard's largest mobilization ever for a natural disaster. It included more than 50,000 citizen-soldiers and airmen from every state, territory, and the District of Columbia and a vast array of aircraft, vehicles, equipment, and supplies. The Guard mounted an unprecedented effort to aid in rescue and recovery efforts, to impose order where lawlessness had broken out, and to provide succor to evacuees. Citizen-soldiers and airmen performed vital rescue work; delivered water, food, and medicine; and helped to clear roads and remove debris. Guard helicopters plucked survivors from the roofs of swamped homes while other state soldiers in small boats and vehicles rescued stranded residents. The National Guard rescued 11,310 people, with 4,200 of them from New Orleans alone. During the last stages of the evacuation from the Crescent City, Guard troops processed 70,000 residents through the Superdome and the Convention Center. In Louisiana alone, the Guard delivered more than 5 million rations, 7 million liters of water, and 12 million pounds of ice. (See figures 4-109 and 4-110.)

The overseas deployment of Gulf Coast Guardsmen raised concerns the National Guard was stretched too thin in the war on terrorism to meet its commitments as both a homeland security force and a federal combat reserve. Even with its full commitment to helping Katrina's victims and to the war on terrorism, the National Guard still possessed nearly 300,000 uncommitted citizen-soldiers and airmen for use wherever they might be needed. "National Guard deployments to Iraq did not slow the Guard's response to Hurricane Katrina," declared Lt. Gen. H. Steven Blum, the chief of the National Guard Bureau. "The fact that National Guard units were deployed to Iraq at the time of Katrina did not lessen the Guard's ability respond." (See figure 4-111.)

After the storm passed, the National Guard remained on the Gulf Coast to help the region recover. While citizens in the hardest-hit remote locations were still without essential services, state soldiers continued to deliver food, water, and medical care. Engineers with heavy equipment removed debris while others helped restore utilities and communications. They paid special attention to schools, with Guard members cleaning up and repairing local schools so communities could regain some degree of normalcy. With the initial recovery phase now completed, the Guard still

4-111 Hurricane Katrina resulted in the largest deployment ever for National Guard personnel responding to a domestic natural disaster. Lt. Gen. H. Steven Blum, Chief, NGB, visits with National Guard personnel deployed to the Gulf Coast at the height of the emergency. NGB

applies its skills as needed during the Gulf Coast's long rebuilding phase.

As the fifth year of the war on terrorism begins, America still depends on the National Guard for safety and security. An offshoot of the war on terrorism has been an increasing concern among the American people over the flood of illegal immigrants, particularly from south of the border. In May 2006, President Bush authorized the deployment of National Guard personnel to buttress the U.S. Customs and Border Patrol until that organization can increase its numbers and improve its capabilities to

provide a more secure border. As part of Operation Jump Start, the Guard has already deployed as many as 6,000 troops to the southwest border. While not directly involved with law enforcement, Guardsmen will perform aerial reconnaissance of the border region and participate in constructing and maintaining roads, fences, light sets, towers, and sensing equipment. (See figure 4-112.)

## The ARNG in Review
Building on its historical roots as the militia and the National Guard, the modern ARNG underwent a period of profound

transformation in the last half of the twentieth century. Emerging from the victory of World War II, the ARNG expanded into a 350,000-strong organization of highly trained and motivated men and women who together have made it the most capable military reserve component in the world. At the same time, ARNG service has remained a volunteer effort, and Guard soldiers have retained their dual status as servants to both the nation and to the states. ARNG soldiers can respond to a wide range of serious threats from major wars to civil disturbances and natural disasters. The Army Guard continues to play an important role in the war on terrorism by defeating America's enemies abroad and by engaging in homeland security missions at home designed to protect the American people. (See figure 4-113.)

Throughout the nation's history, citizen-soldiers have risen up to confront and defeat evil. Two hundred years ago, colonial minutemen rushed from their plows to take up their muskets whenever danger approached. Today's Guard soldiers uphold that special heritage by taking up arms to confront and overcome the clear and present dangers confronting the nation at the beginning of the twenty-first century. If history is any indicator, the ARNG will be more than equal to the task.

4-112 National Guard members man a border surveillance post at Johnson Mountain, New Mexico, in June 2006 as part of Operation Jump Start. The team gathers intelligence about possible undocumented aliens attempting to enter the United States from Mexico and relays it to Border Patrol agents. The skybox provides a higher vantage point and contains optics and electronics that enhance day and night observation. NGB

4-113 The ARNG Readiness Center in Arlington, Virginia, serves as the Army Guard's national headquarters. NGB

# FIVE

# The Air National Guard, 1946–2006

## The Birth of a New Air Arm

**D**espite the important contributions of National Guard flying units and aviators during World War II, the AAF generals who fought for an independent Air Force following the war placed little faith in citizen-airmen. Leaders of the AAF, like General Henry H. "Hap" Arnold, were determined to build the largest and most modern Air Force possible based on nuclear-capable, heavy bombers. Those same leaders were convinced that citizen-airmen could only operate and maintain complex, modern aircraft after receiving extensive training following the declaration of a national emergency. To AAF leaders, state airmen had no place in a new Air Force.

After considerable wrangling in the Pentagon and in Congress, Air Force leaders reluctantly accepted the establishment of a separate air arm of the National Guard. Austere defense budgets after 1945 precluded the creation of a robust Air Force, and citizen-airmen were essential to providing the balance of the nation's air

5-1 The cover of the first monthly issue of *National Guardsman* featured an Air Guard air traffic controller. NGEF

5-2 RF-51s of Tennessee's 155th Reconnaissance Squadron. NGEF

assets. Planners envisioned the creation of twelve National Guard wing headquarters, twenty-four fighter groups, twelve aircraft control and warning organizations, fourteen antiaircraft artillery brigades, and three light bomb groups. In January 1946 the National Guard received authority to activate state flying units. The Air Guard's first personnel and equipment consisted of World War II veteran pilots and propeller-driven fighters and light bombers. The first unit organized in the entire National Guard following World War II was Colorado's 120th Fighter Squadron, which was activated on June 30, 1946. (See figures 5-1 and 5-2.)

The National Security Act of 1947 reorganized the postwar Pentagon and created the independent U.S. Air Force (USAF). On September 18, 1947, the Air Force officially became a separate service. On the same day, the Air National Guard (ANG) came into being. The ANG included 70 percent of the USAF's interceptors, and its primary mission was the air defense of CONUS. Despite

5-3 B-26 "Invaders" of New York's 106th Bombardment Group. NGEF

5-4 In 1948 five ANG squadrons converted from piston-engine to jet aircraft, including Nebraska's 173d Fighter Squadron (Jet) flying F-80C "Shooting Stars." NENG

made the ANG's first years difficult. Many USAF senior officers considered ANG units as little more than state-sponsored flying clubs. Yet, the ANG finally established its own identity distinct from its former role as an appendage of National Guard ground combat units. By 1950 the ANG consisted of seventy-two fighter and twelve light bomber squadrons, and its nonflying elements included thirty-six air contol and warning units. The ANG inventory numbered more than 2,400 aircraft, including 211 jet fighters, and its personnel strength stood at nearly 45,000 airmen. (See figures 5-3 and 5-4.)

## The Korean War, 1950–1953

While only one-third of the ARNG participated in the Korean War, some 80 percent of the ANG became directly involved. Guard airmen contributed significantly to the air war in Korea and to the USAF's global buildup for a possible war with the Soviet Union. A total of sixty-six squadrons were mobilized; fifty remained

its new status, poor relations with the Air Force, limited budgets, recruiting difficulties, and obsolescent aircraft and equipment

5-5 F-84 "Thunderjets" of the 116th Fighter-Bomber Wing enroute to Japan in 1951. NGEF

5-6 A squadron of F-84s of the 136th Fighter-Bomber Wing on a bombing mission over Korea. NGEF

stateside, ten went to Europe, and six fought in Korea. Three ANG fighter squadrons, the 111th (Texas), 182nd (Texas), and the 154th (Arkansas), were formed into the all-ANG 136th Fighter-Bomber Group. The 136th began operations from Japan in June 1951 and moved to a forward base in Korea in October. The 116th Fighter-Bomber Wing, made up of the 158th (Georgia), 159th (Florida), and the 196th (California) Squadrons, arrived in Japan shortly after the 136th. To increase their flying time over Korea, these ANG squadrons became the first in the USAF to experiment with in-flight jet refueling in combat. ANG pilots flew 39,530 combat sorties and destroyed thirty-nine enemy aircraft. Four ANG pilots achieved the coveted status of ace. But the Air Guard's achievements in Korea came with a high price; in all, 101 Air Guardsmen died during the war. (See figures 5-5 through 5-13).

5-7 Airman First Class Story J. Sloane of the 136th Fighter-Bomber Wing refuels an F-84 at Taegu, Korea. **NGB**

5-8 Final preflight check before a pilot leaves on a sortie in Korea. **NGB**

**5-9 First Lt. Bruce McMahan (left) of Texas's 182d Fighter-Bomber Squadron, 136th Fighter-Bomber Wing, is being interviewed by the Wing's commander upon completion of McMahan's 100th sortie over enemy territory, 1952. NGEF**

**5-10 An Air Force reporter interviews the ground crew of the F-84 aircraft "Miss Jacque II" used by Lieutenant McMahan to fly his 100th mission over Korea. NGEF**

## Lessons Learned from Korea

The Korean War was a turning point for the ANG. Despite the accomplishments of individual pilots and ANG units, the war clearly demonstrated that closer harmony between the USAF and the ANG was needed. In subsequent years the ANG acquired specific wartime missions, became more closely involved with Air Force missions on a daily basis, and met the same tough training standards as active-duty units. The primary aim of all these reforms was to make the ANG combat ready the moment it was ordered to active duty. The ANG led the way in altering National Guard drill periods from four separate weeknights each month to a single, long weekend every four weeks. The ANG fought hard to acquire modern aircraft and facilities and transformed itself from a disjointed flying club to a combat-ready, reserve component of the USAF. (See figures 5-14 through 5-17.)

In 1953 the Air Force approved an Air Guard proposal for the Runway Alert Program in which ANG fighters stood alert

5-11 An F-84 of the 116th Fighter-Bomber Wing refuels in air en route to a bombing mission over Korea. NGB

5-12 A pilot of the 127th Fighter-Bomber Squadron (KS) is escorted to his F-84C by his sons as he prepares to deploy to France during the Korean War. NGEF

5-13 Among the ten ANG squadrons deployed to Europe during the Korean War was the 167th Fighter-Bomber Wing (WV) serving in England. NGEF

5-14 The ANG has units that adopt special ceremonial dress, such as the 561st Air Force Band (CA) in 1951. NGEF

5-15 A C-47 "Gooney Bird" of Utah's 151st Support Squadron. NGEF

5-16 Snow-stranded cattle receive an emergency hay drop from a Wyoming C-47. NGEF

5-17 Starting in the 1950s, the ANG received large sums of money to construct modern facilities. NGEF

5-18 Pilots of Nebraska's 173d Fighter Interceptor Squadron dash to their planes during the Runway Alert Program. NENG

against Soviet bombers threatening the American homeland. The first ANG units involved included two fighter squadrons at Haywood, California, and Hancock Field at Syracuse, New York. Pilots and aircraft stood alert from one hour before daylight until one hour after sundown. The program was one of the ANG's greatest successes, and by 1961 it included twenty-five fighter squadrons on alert at key selected airfields on a round-the-clock basis. The Runway Alert Program marked the beginning of the Air Force's integrated approach to the training and employment of its Air Guard and Air Force Reserve assets. (See figures 5-18 and 5-19.)

## The Berlin Crisis

By 1960 ANG personnel strength had grown to 71,000, and its force structure included tactical fighter, reconnaissance, troop carrier, heavy airlift, refueling, and aeromedical evacuation units. Its fighter inventory now consisted entirely of jets, including F-104s, F-100s, F-84s, and F-89Js. (See figures 5-20, 5-21, and 5-22.)

Like the Army Guard, ANG units were mobilized after the Soviet Union began construction of a formidable wall that split Berlin. A total of 21,000 Air Guardsmen were mobilized in the fall of 1961. In a show of resolve, President John F. Kennedy dispatched eleven ANG fighter squadrons to Europe. During October and November 1961, eight of the squadrons flew to

5-19 With most alerts at night, these pilots of the 168th Fighter-Bomber Squadron (IL) scramble to man their F-84s. NGEF

5-20 To enhance recruitment in the mid-1950s, the ANG orga-nized a precision flying team called the "Minute Men" from Colorado's 140th Fighter-Interceptor Wing, flying their F-84s. NGEF

5-21 By the late 1950s, the ANG started flying Korean War vintage F-86 "Sabre Jets" like these of California's 115th Fighter-Interceptor Squadron. NGEF

Europe in Operation Stair Step, the largest jet deployment in ANG history. Because pilots were not trained and their aircraft were not configured for aerial refueling, the squadrons island-hopped across the Atlantic Ocean. All aircraft arrived safely in Europe without a single accident or loss. During the Korean War, ANG units had taken as long as seven months to reach the war zone, but in 1961 they were in Europe within thirty days of mobilization. The majority of Air Guardsmen remained in the United States

preparing for wartime missions in case the crisis escalated into open warfare. The Soviets eventually backed down, and by the late summer of 1962, all Guardsmen had returned home. (See figures 5-23, 5-24, and 5-25).

Despite its overall success in the Berlin Crisis, the ANG fell short of realizing its full potential as a fighting force. After mobilization, Air Guard units in general required substantial additional training, personnel augmentation, and equipment infusions. The USAF lacked spare parts to support aging F-84s and F-86s and did not have plans to employ Guard units short of a major war with the Soviets. NGB realized that the ANG needed newer aircraft, increased funding, additional manpower, and better planning to reach its full development and turned to Congress and the USAF to acquire the needed resources. (See figures 5-26 through 5-32.)

## The Cuban Missile Crisis

A showdown between the United States and the Soviet Union over the deployment of communist ballistic missiles and strategic bombers to Cuba pushed the world to the brink of nuclear war.

The Cuban Missile Crisis of October 1962 included Air Guard involvement. Several ANG squadrons were alerted for mobilization and placed in an accelerated training status, but none saw active duty. Air Guard air defense alert commitments from Puerto Rico were increased, and volunteer

5-22 The 176th Fighter-Interceptor Squadron (WI) flying F-89J "Scorpion" fighters in 1961. NGEF

5-23 In the early 1960s the ANG received more modern aircraft, including the F-104A "Starfighter," which required pilots to don special high-pressure suits. These members of South Carolina's 157th Fighter-Interceptor Squadron deployed with their F-104s to Germany during the Berlin Crisis. NGEF

5-25 An ANG military policeman guards F-84F aircraft of the 149th Fighter-Interceptor Squadron (VA) parked at Byrd Field, Richmond, in 1962. VANG

5-24 Pilots of the 110th Tactical Fighter Squadron (MO) receive a briefing prior to their deployment to France in 1961. NGEF

5-26 Starting in the 1960s, all new ANG enlistees attended active Air Force basic training. This flight, composed of Guardsmen from four states, is being trained at Parks Air Force Base, CA. NGEF

5-27 A pilot of North Dakota's 119th Fighter Group gets "rescued" from the water during survival training in 1963. NGEF

5-28 Capt. Craig Iverson from the 140th Tactical Fighter Wing (CO) practices water survival techniques while awaiting "rescue" in 1966. NGEF

ANG crews flew more than two dozen airlift missions before the emergency ended. Fearful of a surprise Soviet nuclear strike against the American homeland, the Air Force dispersed many of its bombers and interceptors to ANG installations. The Air Guard established and manned command posts to operate those installations on a continuous basis. The crisis ended in November 1962 after the Soviets agreed to dismantle their missile sites and withdraw their bombers from Cuba.

## The McNamara Reforms

Just as the tenure of Secretary of Defense Robert S. McNamara saw significant changes and enhancements of the relationship between the Army and the ARNG, the early 1960s saw increased teamwork between the USAF and the ANG. The clearest demonstration of the ANG's newfound capabilities was the successful outcome of Operation Ready Go, an initiative designed to test the ability of aircraft to deploy more rapidly to NATO. The first quick deployment came in August 1964, when F-100s of the District of Columbia ANG and RF-84s of the Alabama ANG deployed to Europe for their annual, two-week training period. Refueled by twenty-eight Air Guard tankers from Illinois, Ohio, and Wisconsin, thirty-one ANG fighter and reconnaissance aircraft crossed the Atlantic in ten hours and were available for duty only forty-five minutes after their

5-29 T.Sgt. Allen MacNeil instructs Capt. John Kenny on the proper use of the .45-caliber Colt pistol in 1963. Both are members of the 157th Military Airlift Group (NH). NGEF

5-31 A Guard radar officer guides interceptors to their targets. NGEF

5-30 Two pilots of Iowa's 132d Fighter-Interceptor Wing examine a target drone they shot down while flying their F-89Js. NGEF

5-32 To give ANG pilots up-to-date weather information, each flying unit has its own Weather Flight to provide the latest forecast. NGEF

arrival in Europe. It was the first time ANG fighters had flown across the Atlantic nonstop and stood in stark contrast to the slower deployment during the Berlin Crisis just two years earlier. (See figures 5-33, 5-34, and 5-35.)

For the first time, the ANG inventory included heavy, multi-engine aircraft. The Air Force had never allocated four-engine transports to the reserve components, but in January 1960 it transferred C-97 Stratocruisers to the ANG. By the end of 1965, the Air Guard's long-range transport fleet had grown to 159 C-97s and 53 C-121 Super Constellations. During the first six months of 1965 alone, the ANG transport fleet carried 85,373 passengers and 16,638 tons of cargo. The Air Guard entered the air refueling business in 1961 with the acquisition of KC-97 tankers. With the ability to extend the range of its own aircraft, ANG tactical fighter units for the first time began to

**5-33** Five F-84Fs of the 178th Tactical Fighter Group (OH) being readied for air-to-air gunnery training. NGEF

**5-34** Ordnance specialists of the 118th Tactical Fighter Squadron (CT) load a Sidewinder missile on an F-100, 1965. NGEF

**5-35** KC-97 air tankers of the Illinois ANG refuel F-100 fighters of the 121st Fighter Squadron (Washington, DC) over Santiago, Spain, during Operation Ready Go, 1964. NGEF

5-36 A C-97 "Stratofreighter" from Delaware moves cargo in the early 1960s. NGEF

5-37 In 1967 a KC-97L tanker of the 136th Air Refueling Wing (TX) is in position to refuel an Air Force F-111. NGEF

5-38 One of the C-121C "Super Constellations" of the 150th Air Transport Squadron (NJ) arrives in the Dominican Republic with supplies to support the American intervention in 1965. NGEF

## Maj. Gen. Winston P. Wilson: The First Air Guard Chief

Winston P. Wilson began a long, successful National Guard career as a mechanic with the 154th Observation Squadron, Arkansas National Guard, in 1929. He was commissioned as a second lieutenant in 1940 and entered active duty that same year as part of the Guard's call-up for World War II. During the war, he served in Washington, D.C., and in the Pacific, where he was assigned as the assistant photo officer, Far East Forces.

"Wimpy" Wilson came to the National Guard Bureau in 1950 and remained there for twenty-one years. In 1953 he became chief of the National Guard Air Division. Wilson believed ANG units should be measured and trained under the same criteria as Air Force units. He integrated the ANG into USAF operations, including the Runway Alert Program. He also converted the ANG from weekly drills to extended weekend drill periods, a pattern later adopted by all reserve components. At Wilson's urging, the ANG received its first multiengine transports that permitted worldwide deployments.

In 1963 governors from fifty-one states and territories nominated Wimpy Wilson at CNGB. The first Air Guardsman appointed to head the entire National Guard, he emphasized better mobility and increased readiness while leading the Guard through the difficult 1960s. He served as CNGB for eight years until his retirement in 1971. Wilson returned home to Forrest City, Arkansas, and retained an interest in National Guard matters until his death on December 31, 1996.

deploy outside CONUS for their annual, active-duty training. Additionally, ANG refueling units began supporting USAF operations worldwide. (See figures 5-36 through 5-39.)

## The Vietnam War

Though President Johnson had refused to mobilize the Guard and the Reserves for the buildup in Vietnam, the ANG's new refueling and transport capabilities resulted in important early support to the war effort. In August 1965 ANG units began flying aeromedical evacuation flights from South Vietnam, and that December volunteer Guard crews flew more than 409 tons of Christmas gifts and mail to U.S. servicemen already serving in country. Between January 1966 and July 1967, Air Guardsmen flew an average of 150 support missions

**5-39 Airmen of New Mexico's ANG repair radio equipment during annual training, 1967. NGEF**

**5-40 Maj. Gen. Winston P. Wilson. NGEF**

each month to Southeast Asia.

In the aftermath of the *Pueblo* crisis and the Tet Offensive in early 1968, the ANG participated in President Johnson's reserve component call-up. Altogether approximately 10,600 Air Guardsmen entered active duty. While most Guard airmen were assigned to strengthen the USAF's depleted strategic reserves, four fighter squadrons deployed to Vietnam. In May 1968 F-100s from the 120th Tactical Fighter Squadron (Colorado) arrived at Phan Rang Air Base, and by June 1, all of the 120th's pilots were flying combat missions. In the meantime, Iowa's 174th, New Mexico's 188th, and New York's 136th fighter squadrons deployed to Vietnam. In addition, the Air Force's 355th Tactical Fighter Squadron drew 85 percent of its personnel from ANG volunteers. The Air Force quickly and effectively integrated ANG squadrons into combat operations. Before they returned home in April 1969, Air Guard pilots and aircraft flew nearly 30,000 sorties while accumulating 50,000 combat flying hours. Seven ANG pilots and one intelligence officer were killed by enemy fire, and three Air Guardsmen were missing in action. At the same time, two ANG fighter squadrons—the 166th (Ohio) and the 127th (Kansas)—deployed to South Korea to help stabilize the situation there during the *Pueblo* crisis. (See figures 5-41 through 5-49.)

5-42 Maj. Albert Shean of the 165th Tactical Reconnaissance Squadron (KY) prepares to take his F-101 "Voodoo" on patrol over the Panama Canal Zone before deploying to Japan in 1968. NGEF

5-41 Pilots of the 165th Tactical Reconnaissance Squadron (KY) enter active duty during the *Pueblo* crisis. NGEF

5-43 An officer of Ohio's 166th Tactical Fighter Squadron discusses his mission with a South Korean Air Force Operations specialist while the unit was stationed at Kunsan Air Base, Korea, 1968. NGEF

Even as the United States waged war in Vietnam, it aggressively pursued the exploration of space with the ultimate goal of placing a man on the moon. Among the astronaut corps were thirteen former members of the ANG. Of these, six eventually flew in space. Two members of the crew for the near-disastrous Apollo 13 mission were former Air Guard members. (See figures 5-50 and 5-51.)

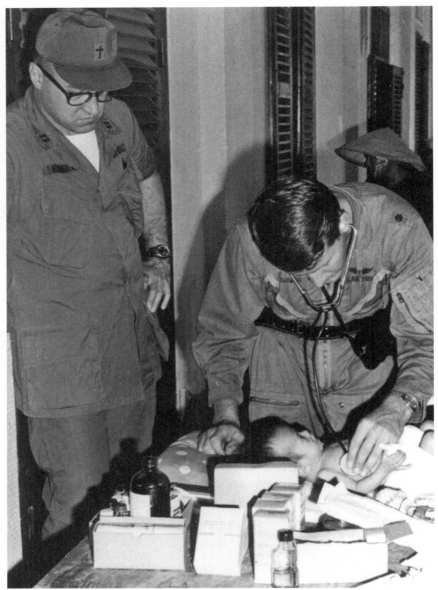

5-44 Flight Surgeon/Maj. Gerald McGowan of Iowa's 174th Tactical Fighter Squadron treats an orphaned Vietnamese child at Phu Cat Air Base, Vietnam. NGEF

## The All-Volunteer Force

Following the end of America's involvement in Vietnam in 1973, substantial reductions in the active Air Force resulted in an infusion into the ANG of newer and more modern aircraft, including A-7s, A-10s, F-105s, OA-37s, and C-130s. But the USAF's principle fighter aircraft, the F-4 Phantom, had logged many flying hours, including

combat operations in Vietnam, before they came to the Guard. The ANG's personnel strength stood at over 90,300 by the end of the Vietnam War. (See figures 5-52 through 5-55.)

The end of the draft and the adoption of the Total Force Policy in the early 1970s prompted closer coordination between the USAF and

the ANG. Henceforth, the ANG was to be the first and primary source of manpower to augment the active Air Force in any future crisis. Perhaps the best example of increased USAF-ANG cooperation was Operation Creek Party, which placed Air Guard tanker aircraft at the disposal of active air commanders in Europe. Between

5-47 The F-100 flown by Capt. Michael Adams of the 188th Tactical Fighter Squadron (NM) returning to Tuy Hoa Air Base, Vietnam. Days after this picture was taken, the plane was shot down and Adams became one of the seven ANG pilots killed in the war. NGEF

5-45 Mobilized with the 185th Fighter-Bomber Squadron (OK) during the Korean War, Lt. Col. James R. Risner served in combat as a replacement, becoming an "ace" with eight kills. Staying in the Regular Air Force, he led numerous bombing missions over North Vietnam, for which he was awarded the first Air Force Cross after its creation in 1965. Soon afterward he was shot down and held as a POW for seven years. NGEF

5-48 As the war in Vietnam grew more unpopular, many CONUS air bases received threats of sabotage. Members of the Air Police of the 183d Combat Support Squadron (IL) practice an alert in 1968. NGEF

5-46 Lt. Col. David Quinlan of New Mexico's 188th Tactical Fighter Squadron returns for debriefing after a mission over North Vietnam, 1969. NGEF

5-49 Air police of the 146th Military Airlift Wing (CA) hold a belligerent demonstrator for the civilian police during an antiwar protest in 1968. NGEF

the start of the program in 1967 and its termination a decade later, hardly a week passed when ANG KC-97Ls were not in the skies over Europe refueling USAF aircraft. Guard refueling groups that were deployed to Rhein-Main Air Base in West Germany as part of their annual training sustained the ANG's long-term European presence. Refueling crews conducted 6,512 accident-free sorties, completed 47,207 hook-ups, and off-loaded 137.4 million pounds of fuel. More significantly, Creek Party showed that the Air Guard could sustain operational rotations overseas short of a national mobilization ordered by the president. (See figures 5-56 through 5-59.)

The end of the draft in 1973 prompted the ANG to increase the participation of minorities to maintain acceptable strength levels. An influx of pilots leaving the post-Vietnam Air Force helped

5-50 Former Massachusetts Air Guardsman Capt. Russell Schweickart set a number of space first's during Apollo 9 in March 1969. The most important was his space walk to test the self-contained suit developed for use in the lunar landings. NASA

5-51 Capt. John Swigert (CT) was one of two former ANG pilots on Apollo 13 in April 1970. NASA

5-52 Colorado's 120th Tactical Fighter Squadron flies their A-7D "Corsair II" aircraft. NGEF

5-53 F-102 "Delta Dagger" supersonic planes flown by the 147th Fighter Group (TX). NGEF

5-54 Two Guard ordnance specialists load missiles inside an F-102 "Delta Dagger" of the 118th Fighter Squadron (CT). NGEF

5-56 A cargo-hauling C-124 "Globemaster" of the 157th Military Airlift Group (NH). NGEF

5-57 Once the ANG received C-130 "Hercules" cargo planes, it could offer direct tactical combat support to ground forces. NGEF

5-55 A F-106B "Delta Dart" of the Montana ANG in 1972. NGEF

5-58 Two airmen maintain a communications link. NGEF

5-59 This member of the 132d Tactical Fighter Squadron (ME), dressed in period costume, celebrates the bicentennial of the American Revolution in 1976. NGEF

5-60 Capt. Norma Parsons. NGB

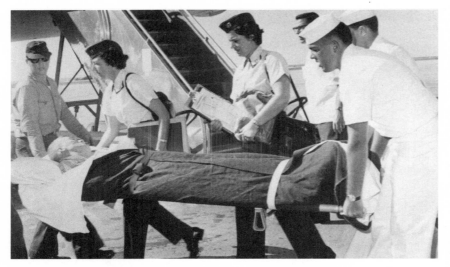

5-61 During the Vietnam War, ANG nurses flew on Aero Medical Evacuation flights returning injured men from hospitals in Japan to stateside treatment facilities. NGEF

to keep cockpits filled, but the Guard still needed additional personnel support. In October 1956 Capt. Norma Parsons of New York became the first woman to join the National Guard. Initially, only nurse positions were open to females, and not until 1968 were women able to serve in nonmedical positions. Women were able to attend flight training starting in 1976. Two years later, 2d Lt. Marilyn Koon of Arizona's 161st Air-Refueling Group pinned on her silver wings to become the ANG's first female pilot. In 1974 the ANG included 1,227 women, or just over 1 percent of its total strength. In the following decade, the presence of Air Guard women increased ten-fold. A similar pattern developed in the recruitment of blacks, Hispanics, and other minorities. In 1971 minority participation accounted for just over 2.5 percent of the ANG. The senior leaders of NGB and the ANG put a high priority on minority recruiting throughout the 1970s. By the end of the decade, racial minorities numbered 12,856 and accounted for nearly 14 percent of the Air Guard. (See figures 5-60 through 5-67.)

## The Reagan Buildup
For the ANG, the eight-year presidency of Ronald Reagan was

5-62 Sgt. Marsha Rivers was the first enlisted woman in the Puerto Rico ANG. NGEF

5-63 Airman First Class Janet Okamoto (CA) operates a ground-to-air radio circuit of an AN/TSW-7 Air Traffic Control Center, 1975. NGEF

5-64 By the mid-1970s ANG women were working in a wide range of specialties. Members of the 119th Fighter-Interceptor Group (ND) set a record by completely loading all of the ordnance on a fighter in less than nineteen minutes. NGEF

5-65 Second Lt. Marilyn Koon, 1978. NGB

5-66 Unlike the Army Guard, which had separate black-only units until the 1960s, the ANG from its creation accepted African Americans in its ranks. This member of New Jersey's 119th Fighter Squadron is working on an F-51 engine in 1954. NGB

5-67 An African-American pilot of the 121st Tactical Fighter Squadron (Washington, DC) stands by his F-4C "Phantom" fighter in 1981. DCNG

a time of expansion and better integration with the Air Force. From a force of 93,379 airmen in 1979, the ANG increased to 117,786 personnel. During the same period, the number of units grew from 1,089 to 1,339. The real increases occurred as flying squadrons raised the number of primary authorized aircraft and the number of support units grew. Like the ARNG, the 1980s saw an increase in ANG minority participation. In December 1982 Brig. Gen. Russell C. Davis assumed command of the 113th Tactical Fighter Wing of the District of Columbia ANG and became the first African American to attain general officer rank in the Air Guard.

As the ANG expanded its integration with the Air Force, the air mobility mission became more important. Compared to earlier decades when the ANG had primarily been a fighter organization, by the late 1980s it was a balanced force capable of diverse missions that included ninety squadrons of airlift, fighter, attack, reconnaissance, special operations, and rescue units. The C-5 Galaxy and C-141 Starlifter entered the inventory, and KC-135 refueling units flew longer deployments. (See figures 5-68 through 5-72.)

An assortment of unit types enabled the ANG to participate in a wide variety of training and operational missions. Fighter pilots trained at Red Flag, the Air Force's realistic, force-on-force air combat school at Nellis Air Force Base, Nevada. Airlift crews flew missions to Europe, the Middle East, and Central America. In 1986 a Guard tanker refueled U.S. bombers during air strikes against Libya. Three years later, the ANG flew airlift, fighter-bomber, and special operations missions during the invasion of

Panama. Aircraft from the 180th (Ohio) and the 114th (South Dakota) Tactical Fighter Groups were the first ANG units to fly combat missions since Vietnam. (See figures 5-73 and 5-74.)

While the ARNG became involved in nation building and

5-68 Each ANG base has its own firefighting equipment and highly trained personnel on twenty-four-hour duty. **NGB**

5-69 ANG firemen often aid civilian airport fire crews when nonmilitary aircraft disasters occur. For instance, in 1984 the fire detachment of the 176th Airlift Group (AK) at Kulis Air Force Base helped extinguish a burning DC-10, which crashed while trying to land. **NGEF**

5-70 The EC-130Es issued to Pennsylvania's 193d Electronic Combat Squadron in the late 1970s were specialized to monitor enemy radio traffic. The unit was deployed during the Persian Gulf War and is the only such unit in the U.S. Air Force. PANG

5-71 The ANG received C-5 "Galaxy" cargo planes in the late 1980s. NGB

5-72 As part of the Reagan buildup, the ANG received the C-141 "Starlifter" in the late 1980s. NGB

5-73 An F-16 of Florida's 159th Fighter-Interceptor Squadron watches a Soviet "Bear" bomber along the East Coast in the waning days of the Cold War. NGEF

defense programs in Central America, the ANG participated in several air support initiatives to the region. Starting in 1978, ANG fighter units provided the air defense of the Panama Canal as part of project Coronet Cove. The U.S. Southern Command, responsible for U.S. operations in Latin America and the Caribbean, relied on ANG C-130 transports for theater airlift as part of Operation Volant Oak. ANG C-130s flew regularly scheduled and special assignment air missions throughout Latin America.

## The Persian Gulf War

On August 6, 1990, four days after the Iraqi army invaded Kuwait, President George Bush announced Operation Desert Shield, the buildup of Allied forces in the

Persian Gulf. Even before the commencement of the reserve component mobilization that came two weeks later, 1,300 ANG personnel volunteered for duty. Air Guard KC-135 aircraft and volunteer aircrews deployed immediately to the Persian Gulf region to support the movement of U.S. forces there. Eventually, twelve of the ANG's thirteen air refueling units contributed sixty-two KC-135 tankers to the war effort. New York's 137th Military Airlift Squadron equipped with the C-5A and Mississippi's 183d Military Airlift Squadron flying the C-141 were the first airmen to volunteer for missions in support of the war effort. (See figure 5-75.)

Placing a large force in Saudi Arabia would be impossible without the reserve components,

so on August 22 President Bush called up Guardsmen and reservists in the largest mobilization since the Korean War. Two days later, the 183d (Mississippi) and the 137th (New York) Military Airlift Squadrons were the first ANG units mobilized and concentrated on airlifting U.S. ground troops to the Persian Gulf region. A total of five ANG Tactical Airlift Groups—166th (Delaware), 139th (Missouri), 136th (Texas), 130th (West Virginia), and a composite volunteer unit— employed their eighty C-130s to provide valuable intratheater airlift. Air Guard tankers pumped more than 250 million pounds of fuel into more than 18,000 aircraft. Cargo planes transported 55,000 personnel and 115,000 tons of equipment and supplies.

The Air Force called upon ANG combat units, and the 169th Tactical Fighter Group (South Carolina) and the 174th Tactical Fighter Wing (New York) equipped with the F-16 Flying Falcon went to the Gulf. Guard fighters participated in the air campaign from the very first day and eventually flew 3,645 missions while dropping 3,500 tons of ordnance. Nevada's 152d Tactical Reconnaissance Group equipped with the RF-4 conducted more than 1,000 tactical reconnaissance missions. (See figures 5-76 through 5-81.)

Altogether 12,404 Air Guardsmen entered active duty during the war. The mobilization included a number of important firsts. Of the total number of personnel mobilized, only 1,160 were in combat formations. For the first time in ANG history, the majority of personnel mobilized were not members of combat flying units. Moreover, the preponderance of Air Guardsmen did not belong to any type of flying unit. The majority of ANG personnel mobilized incorporated a wide variety of units, including medical and aeromedical evacuation, security police, services, firefighters, mobile aerial ports, communications, and engineers.

**5-74 A pilot of the 174th Tactical Fighter Squadron, based at Sioux City, IA, carries an injured child from the burning wreckage of United Airlines Flight 232, which crashed on the field on July 19, 1989. NGEF**

**5-75 En route to the Persian Gulf an F-16C "Falcon" fighter of the 169th Tactical Fighter Group (SC) gets refueled by a KC-135 tanker flown by Tennessee's 151st Air Refueling Wing. NGB**

5-76 A pilot of the 174th Tactical Fighter Wing (NY) walks to his F-16C during Desert Storm. NGB

5-77 Capt. Ross Swezey, Weapons Systems Officer, with the 152d Tactical Reconnaissance Group (NV) indicates he's ready for another mission in his RF-4C "Phantom" during Desert Storm. NGB

5-78 Flying supplies to a forward base prior to the start of Desert Storm is a C-130 of Delaware's 166th Airlift Group. NGB

## Downsizing and Adaptation

In the immediate aftermath of the Persian Gulf War, political and military leaders acknowledged the end of the Cold War by putting into motion plans to reduce as much as one-quarter of their troops and equipment. The National Guard's senior leadership in the Pentagon began the challenging process of modestly downsizing and restructuring the Air Guard. At the end of 1991, the ANG stood at an all-time high strength of 117,786 citizen-airmen. Much like the cuts following the Vietnam War, reductions in the Air Force resulted in the fielding of better, more modern aircraft to ANG units. Air Guard pilots took command of F-16 Fighting Falcons, and increasingly sophisticated airlifters and tankers replaced some Vietnam-era aircraft whose age matched that of their crews. (See figure 5-82.)

The ANG successfully adapted to post–Cold War conditions. Instead of eliminating airmen and flying units, personnel attrition and reductions in primary authorized aircraft allowed the Air Guard to achieve lower manning levels. As the active Air Force lost more units, the Air Guard integrated itself more closely into Air Force operations. Many fighter squadrons turned in their sleek jets for tankers and transport aircraft. Heavy bombers also entered the ANG inventory for the first time since the Korean War when the 184th (Kansas) and 116th (Georgia) Bombardment

5-79 A pilot of the 169th Tactical Fighter Group (SC), the "Swamp Foxes" receives a "go" signal from a crew chief that he's ready for takeoff. NGB

5-80 Munitions crew of the 169th CAM Squadron (SC) removing a CBU-52 cluster bomb from a trailer on the flightline at Al Kharj, Saudi Arabia. NGEF

Groups received the B-1 bomber. By 1997 the ANG possessed a large portion of the Air Force's entire capabilities, including 44 percent of tactical airlift, 8 percent of strategic airlift, and 43 percent of air refueling. At the end of the 1990s, the ANG stood at just below 110,000 personnel and possessed forty-two fighter units plus one special operations, three rescue, and two heavy bomber units. In 2000 the ANG provided all of USAF's interceptor forces charged with the air defense of CONUS. At the same time, the ANG received control of the First Air Force, the command

5-81 Two OA-10 "Warthogs" of the 110th Fighter Wings (MI) fly over Kuwait City after its liberation. NGB

5-82 The final flight of two RF-4C "Phantoms" by Nevada's 152d Reconnaissance Group before they were retired in 1995. NGEF

responsible for the air defense of the United States. These capabilities represent a dramatic change from the 1950s when the ANG was almost exclusively a fighter aircraft force. (See figure 5-83.)

At the same time, the ANG continued to seek the best-qualified personnel to fill its ranks. Women and minorities became an even more important presence, especially in senior command positions. In 1997 Maj. Gen. Martha T. Rainville became the AG of Vermont, the first female to hold the position of state AG in the history of the National Guard. The following year, Lt. Gen. Russell C. Davis became the first African American to serve as CNGB. (See figures 5-84 and 5-85.)

## Guardsmen as Peacekeepers

With the end of the Cold War, the strategy of containing communism gave way to peacetime global engagement. Through its involvement in regional crises, the United States hoped to prevent political, ethnic, and racial hatreds from escalating into larger wars. The ANG first demonstrated that Guardsmen made good peacekeepers. In late 1992 Guard airlifters and refuelers flew missions in support of humanitarian relief efforts in Somalia. Before long, Air Guard units were involved in relief operations in Africa, Bosnia, and northern Iraq. In addition, the Air Guard provided crews and C-130s from fourteen units to support the U.S. military intervention in Haiti

5-83 A B-1B bomber of the 184th Bombardment Group (KS). KSNG

5-84 Maj. Gen. Martha Rainville. VTNG

in September 1994 that restored the democratically elected president of that country to power. The Air Guard also supported the enforcement of no-fly zones over northern and southern Iraq after the Persian Gulf War. All these operations confirmed the notion that the ANG had become a regular, active augmentation to the USAF rather than solely a reserve organization.

The Guard's greatest contributions as a peacekeeping force occurred in the Balkans. In August 1994 six ANG tanker units began participation in Operation Deny Flight, the enforcement of a UN–declared no-fly zone over Bosnia. After years of brutal warfare, the states of the former Yugoslavia negotiated a peace in late 1995 that required the presence of NATO peacekeepers. For the next four years, ANG tankers and airlifters were a constant presence over the Balkans in support of U.S. and NATO peacekeepers on the ground. (See figures 5-86 and 5-87.)

In 1999 the Balkan peace mission turned into a shooting war when NATO mounted Operation Allied Force, an aerial campaign designed to stop Serbian aggression in Kosovo. Before the campaign ended, 3,377 ANG personnel and eighty-seven aircraft saw service. Eighteen A-10 Warthogs from the 104th (Massachusetts) and 110th (Michigan) Fighter Wings as well as the 124th Composite Wing (Idaho) saw action over Kosovo. While dropping nearly 600 bombs and shooting over 14,000 rounds of ammunition, ANG pilots fired the National Guard's last shots in anger of the twentieth century.

## The War on Terrorism

Since the 1950s, the ANG has worked with the Air Force to provide for the air defense of CONUS. With the end of the Cold War and the waning specter of a nuclear confrontation with the former Soviet Union, the USAF dedicated fewer and fewer resources to continental defense. In 1997, the Pentagon designated the 1st Air Force at Tyndall Air Force Base in Panama City, Florida, as an Air Guard major command responsible for the nation's air defense. By the end of the twentieth century, the country's active air defense system consisted of only seven alert sites where a total of fourteen fully armed and fueled ANG interceptors sat on constant alert. Backing up the interceptors was the 1st Air Force's command center and three regional air

5-85 Lt. Gen. Russell C. Davis. NGB

5-86 An ANG air crew at work over Bosnia, 1996. NGEF

5-87 M.Sgt. David Leitenberger, 179th Airlift Group (OH) greets a United Nations worker at the Sarajevo Airport, Bosnia, 1995. NGEF

5-88 Two future commanders in chief. George H. W. Bush pins the second lieutenant bars on his son George W. in 1968. The younger Bush flew fighter aircraft in the Texas ANG. NGEF

5-89 President George W. Bush visits with members of the West Virginia National Guard in early 2001. NGB

defense sectors. The expected threat to the homeland remained attacks by aircraft or missiles originating from beyond the nation's borders, and the 1st Air Force's ability to track and defend against any threats within U.S. airspace remained limited.

When terrorists piloted four hijacked commercial airliners in suicide attacks against ground targets on September 11, 2001, the plot represented an unprecedented threat in the history of U.S. continental air defense. Citizen-airmen were the first in the air to respond to the surprise attack. A flight of F-15s from the 102d (Massachusetts) Fighter Wing appeared over lower Manhattan only eight minutes after two airliners slammed into the World Trade Center towers.

Moments after the attack on the Pentagon, an F-16 from North Dakota's 119th Fighter Wing on duty at the alert site at Langley Air Force Base, Virginia, streaked low over the building. The sight of that F-16 gave the badly shaken people on the ground a sense of security because word had spread that a fourth hijacked airliner, which ultimately crashed in rural Pennsylvania, was bearing down on the nation's capital. By noon, ANG fighters from Langley and the District of Columbia had established a combat air patrol over the city. Across the nation, citizen-airmen rushed to their ANG bases to volunteer their services, and ANG fighters helped resolve discrepancies with other possible hijackings and civilian aircraft that had lost contact with air

traffic control. Late that fateful day, interceptors from Texas's 111th Fighter Squadron—President George W. Bush's former Air Guard unit—and the District of Columbia's ANG 121st Fighter Squadron escorted Air Force One as the president returned to Washington, D.C. (See figures 5-88 and 5-89.)

Defending against further aerial terrorist attacks became a key component of Operation Noble Eagle, the new homeland security mission. The Air Force and the ANG mounted a herculean effort to rejuvenate the nation's minimal air defense system, even as interceptors—supported by the ANG aerial refueling fleet— flew near-continuous combat air patrols over the nation's major cities. Over time the need to

5-90 Bristling with armed missiles, an F-16 of the Vermont ANG flies a combat air patrol above the smoldering debris of the World Trade Center on September 12, 2001. NGB

5-91 F-16s of the North Dakota ANG fly over Washington, DC, in the weeks following the terrorist attacks. The damaged Pentagon appears in the left background. NGB

5-92 An F-16 from California's 144th Fighter Wing passes low over the Golden Gate bridge as part of Operation Noble Eagle.

patrol the largest cities receded, but constant combat air patrols were maintained over New York City and Washington, D.C. The clear burden for air defense fell to the ANG, and pilots and aircraft experienced extreme usage rates in the six months following the September 11 attacks. By late 2002, other defense measures had reduced the need for extended combat air patrols, and the active alert sites across the country increased to twenty. As the war on terrorism continues, the ANG remains responsible for air defense and stands on constant alert against unexpected aerial threats. (See figures 5-90 through 5-92.)

Even as ANG fighter and tanker units participated in Operation Noble Eagle, the remainder of the Air Guard became engaged in the overseas portion of the new global war on terrorism. The United States and other coalition forces were bent on attacking the terrorists' stronghold in Afghanistan and needed air power to project forces into the region. In an unprecedented action, the Air Force established two aerial bridges that girdled the globe in both directions from CONUS and converged on the other side of the world in southwest Asia. With extensive assistance from ANG tankers and airlifters, the rapid buildup of forces for OEF occurred quickly. (See figure 5-93.)

ANG units and personnel were in the vanguard of the attack

against the Taliban and al Qaeda. One of the first Air Force units to deploy to combat was Pennsylvania's 193d Special Operations Wing. Equipped with unique EC-130s capable of broadcasting radio and television signals to enemy combatants and civilian populations, the 193d convinced enemy fighters to surrender rather than face the wrath of U.S. firepower. On the ground, ANG combat controllers worked with U.S. and coalition SF personnel and Afghan fighters to rout the enemy in record time. Combat controllers called in devastating precision airstrikes against Taliban and al Qaeda fighters throughout Afghanistan. U.S. senior commanders were particularly concerned about rescuing downed pilots and evacuating wounded SF personnel, and the Air Force searched far and wide for every pararescueman (PJ) available. Kentucky's 123d Special Tactics Squadron had the ANG's inventory of PJs, and the unit's members saw extensive service throughout Afghanistan and in other surrounding areas. (See figures 5-94 and 5-95.)

One of the most intense firefights to date in the global war on terrorism occurred in Afghanistan's high mountains on March 4, 2002. American forces were engaged in heavy fighting in the Hindu Kush Mountains during Operation Anaconda, and commanders wanted to gain an advantage over al Qaeda fighters

5-93 ANG C-130s played an important role in establishing forward operating bases in Uzbekistan, Oman, and other surrounding countries at the beginning of OEF. NGB

5-94 Two F-16 Fighting Falcons from the 149th Fighter Wing (TX) on a mission over Afghanistan. NGB

5-95 Members of Wisconsin's 128th Air Refueling Wing board a KC-135 Stratotanker as part of the deployments for OEF. NGB

5-96 The National Guard Heritage series painting "Takur Ghar" depicts the courage and selfless service of ANG PJ Keary Miller during that fight in Afghanistan, March 2002. NGB

5-97 One of the "Red Devil" F-16s of the 107th Fighter Squadron, 127th Fighter Wing, Michigan ANG taking off from Kirkuk Air Base, Iraq, in March 2004. The squadron nickname of "Red Devils" came from its adoption prior to World War II of a red devil insignia, which was painted upon its aircraft. NGB

by establishing an observation post atop the highest summit in the region, Takur Ghar. When the insertion of an SF observation team went awry, a group of Army Rangers and an Air Force PJ team were dispatched to Takur Ghar. Among the rescuers was T.Sgt. Keary Miller, an experienced PJ from the 123d Special Tactics Squadron. Unfortunately, the helicopter carrying the rescue party came under heavy enemy fire and crashed near Takur Ghar's summit, resulting in several killed and wounded. Mortar and gunfire were too thick to risk another helicopter rescue, so the survivors were ordered to hunker down on the mountain. With little regard for his own safety, Sergeant Miller was instrumental in caring for the wounded and helping others reach a safer and more defensible position

5-98 Maj. James Ewald, an A-10 Warthog pilot from the 172d Fighter Squadron, 110th Fighter Wing, Michigan ANG, was shot down and rescued during Operation Iraqi Freedom on April 8, 2003. NGB

away from the downed helicopter. When darkness finally fell across the mountain, the Americans were extracted with seven killed and eleven wounded. For his gallantry and steadfastness under fire, the

Air Force awarded Miller the Silver Star, the nation's third highest medal for valor. He was the National Guard's first Silver Star recipient since the Vietnam War. (See figure 5-96.)

The opening of OIF in March 2003 placed additional demands on the Air Guard. From the beginning of the Iraq War, the ANG has provided a full spectrum of capabilities. Fighters and ground attack aircraft supported conventional combat operations in the war's first months. Air refuelers and lift aircraft have sustained a continuous air bridge from Iraq to logistics facilities in Kuwait, Germany, and CONUS. An important function of ANG airlifters has been to evacuate the most severely wounded soldiers to vital medical treatment facilities in Germany and CONUS. With more support units available, the Air Guard has taken on additional ground roles in Iraq, especially in providing security for air bases and other key installations. (See figures 5-97 through 5-100.)

Even as the U.S. military prosecutes the campaigns in Afghanistan and Iraq, it is undergoing a process of defense transformation to posture itself for the uncertain challenges of the twenty-first century. Transformation envisions military forces linked in combat by computer networks and advanced sensors that provide a common view of the battlefield for more coordinated and effective attacks using precision-guided munitions.

The National Guard is part of the transformation process already begun by the Army and the Air Force. In 2003, the National Guard launched an initiative to simplify and standardize the command

5-99 Members of the "Kirkuk Seven" standing with enlarged Ace of Spades from the deck of the "Most Wanted" honoring the role they played in the capture of Saddam Hussein. The seven women, all members of the 193d Special Operations Wing, Pennsylvania ANG, had volunteered to work in a medical clinic in Kirkuk treating Iraqi civilians. By December 2003 the quality of their care and concern had built up enough trust among their patients that they were told where to find the former Iraqi leader, leading to his capture. PANG

5-101 A Guard sentry stands his post in front of the JFHQ-California headquarters building as part of Operation Noble Eagle. The transformation of the former state headquarters into joint organizations has helped the National Guard to more effectively perform its federal and state missions. CANG

5-100 Ordnance specialists of South Carolina's 169th CAM Squadron load an AIM-120 AMRAAN missile onto the wing of an F-16 Falcon fighter during the air campaign of OIF, March 2003. NGB

**5-102 Recruiting has been a National Guard priority throughout the war on terrorism. One of the Guard's most effective recruiting tools has been the sponsorship of a race car on the NASCAR circuit. Car Number 16 sits on the tarmac at Andrews Air Force Base, Maryland, before a District of Columbia ANG hangar during an Armed Forces Day celebration. NGB**

structures in each of the fifty-four states and territories. A major goal of the reorganization was to create command structures that senior Army and Air Force commanders could easily recognize and that would speed mobilizations and the flow of resources during national emergencies and natural disasters. The separate, subordinate ARNG and ANG commands that existed in the old state headquarters were merged into a single joint organization akin to the staff structure of the overseas combatant commands and were renamed the Joint Force Headquarters (JFHQ). (See figures 5-101 and 5-102.)

The response to Hurricane Katrina exhibited the advantages of the National Guard's new JFHQ in each state. The disaster generated perhaps the fastest mobilization of the largest number of troops into a single geographic region in American military history. While the ANG performed its traditional mission of airlifting Guard personnel and equipment to the disaster site, Katrina prompted two new airlift missions: the air transport of storm evacuees to other locations throughout the country and the aerial medical evacuation of the injured to treatment facilities outside the Gulf Coast region. Both tasks demonstrated the inherent flexibility of air power and the Air Guard's ability to execute civil support missions. (See figures 5-103 and 5-104.)

The ANG continues to assume more homeland security missions. The president's call in May 2006 to send 6,000 Guardsmen to the nation's southwest border to increase security has included citizen-airmen. ANG security forces have provided detachments and individuals to work with the Border Patrol in support functions. The defense of the homeland will always remain a top national security priority, and the Air Guard will certainly continue to broaden its contributions in defending the American people from direct attacks and protecting them from natural disasters. (See figure 5-105.)

## The ANG in Review

Since 1947 the ANG has served proudly alongside the U.S. Air Force while promoting the concept of the citizen-airman among the American people. Following its reorganization after World War II, the ANG met its first test in Korea, an experience that opened opportunities for needed improvements and closer integration with the active Air Force. Increased federal funding allowed for better training, improved facilities, and more modern aircraft and equipment. Throughout the Cold War, the ANG provided air units to meet major crises and to deter communist aggression around the globe. With the advent of the all-volunteer force in the early 1970s, increased minority participation improved the ANG's ethnic and social diversity. The ANG gradually shifted from an exclusively combat-oriented flying force in the 1950s to one whose units are evenly distributed between combat and combat support missions. The Persian Gulf War demonstrated that ANG units and individual Guardsmen were capable of rapid global deployment

5-103 A Gulf Coast resident shows her thanks for the National Guard's emergency efforts in the aftermath of Hurricane Katrina by hugging an Ohio Guard flyer. NGB

5-104 ANG medical personnel helped to evacuate and treat the many injured from Hurricane Katrina. The 130th Airlift Wing, West Virginia ANG, unloads injured from a C-130H after a flight from Louie Armstrong New Orleans International Airport. NGB

5-105 Border Patrol agents assigned S.Sgt. Dominic Flores, 162d Fighter Wing, Arizona ANG, to a communications center as part of Operation Jump Start because his civilian job as a Tucson police officer suited him perfectly for the task of running criminal record checks. NGB

and of immediately integrating into USAF operations. In the 1990s Air Guardsmen served with distinction in Southwest Asia and in the Balkans during operations fully integrated with the Air Force. After the September 11 attacks, the Air Guard has taken the lead in defending America's skies from other attacks while also playing an important role in OEF and OIF. At the same time, its mix of ground support units has allowed the ANG to become more active in homeland security missions and in responding to natural disasters.

At the beginning of the twenty-first century, the U.S. Air Force and the Air National Guard are complementary. In fact, the USAF relies on the ANG to accomplish many crucial missions. If provided modern equipment, realistic training, and clear-cut missions, the ANG will remain crucial to America's defense needs both at home and abroad. While developing its own capabilities and closer relations with the Air Force in the past decades, the ANG has demonstrated America's citizen-airmen need not take a backseat to any other military airmen in the world.

# APPENDIX
# MAJOR NATIONAL GUARD UNITS

## Army National Guard Units
### Divisions—Headquarters Locations (as of September 30, 2000)

| | |
|---|---|
| 28th Infantry Division (Mechanized) | Pennsylvania |
| 2d Brigade | Pennsylvania |
| 55th Brigade | Pennsylvania |
| 56th Brigade | Pennsylvania |
| Division Artillery | Pennsylvania |
| 28th Aviation Brigade | Pennsylvania |
| 28th Engineer Brigade | Virginia |
| DISCOM | Pennsylvania |
| | |
| 29th Infantry Division (Light) | Virginia |
| 1st Brigade | Virginia |
| 3d Brigade | Maryland |
| 26th Brigade | Massachusetts |
| Division Artillery | Virginia |
| DISCOM | Maryland |
| | |
| 34th Infantry Division (Mechanized) | Minnesota |
| 1st Brigade | Minnesota |
| 2d Brigade | Iowa |
| 32d Brigade | Wisconsin |
| Division Artillery | Minnesota |
| 34th Aviation Brigade | Minnesota |
| DISCOM | Minnesota |
| | |
| 35th Infantry Division (Mechanized) | Kansas |
| 66th Brigade | Illinois |
| 67th Brigade | Nebraska |
| 149th Brigade | Kentucky |
| Division Artillery | Kentucky |
| 35th Aviation Brigade | Missouri |
| DISCOM | Missouri |

| | |
|---|---|
| 38th Infantry Division (Mechanized) | Indiana |
|     2d Brigade | Indiana |
|     37th Brigade | Ohio |
|     46th Brigade | Michigan |
|     Division Artillery | Indiana |
|     38th Aviation Brigade | Indiana |
|     DISCOM | Indiana |
| | |
| 40th Infantry Division (Mechanized) | California |
|     1st Brigade | California |
|     2d Brigade | California |
|     3d Brigade | California |
|     40th Engineer Brigade | California |
|     40th Aviation Brigade | California |
|     DISCOM | California |
| | |
| 42d Infantry Division (Mechanized) | New York |
|     3d Brigade | New York |
|     50th Brigade | New Jersey |
|     86th Brigade | Vermont |
|     42d Engineer Brigade | New York |
|     42d Aviation Brigade | New York |
|     DISCOM | New Jersey |
| | |
| 49th Armored Division | Texas |
|     36th Brigade | Texas |
|     2d Brigade | Texas |
|     3d Brigade | Texas |
|     49th Engineer Brigade | Texas |
|     49th Aviation Brigade | Texas |
|     DISCOM | Texas |
| | |
| Combat Brigades | |
|     27th Infantry Brigade (Light) | New York |
|     29th Infantry Brigade | Hawaii |
|     30th Infantry Brigade (Mechanized) | North Carolina |
|     39th Infantry Brigade | Arkansas |
|     41st Infantry Brigade | Oregon |
|     45th Infantry Brigade | Oklahoma |
|     48th Infantry Brigade (Mechanized) | Georgia |
|     53d Infantry Brigade | Florida |
|     76th Infantry Brigade | Indiana |
|     81st Infantry Brigade (Mechanized) | Washington |
|     92d Infantry Brigade (Separate) | Puerto Rico |

| | |
|---|---|
| 218th Infantry Brigade (Mechanized) | South Carolina |
| 256th Infantry Brigade (Mechanized) | Louisiana |
| 31st Armored Brigade (Separate) | Alabama |
| 116th Cavalry Brigade | Idaho/Oregon/ Montana/Wyoming |
| 155th Armored Brigade | Mississippi |

Armored Cavalry Regiment
| | |
|---|---|
| 278th Armored Cavalry Regiment | Tennessee |

Major Separate Headquarters Units
| | |
|---|---|
| I Corps Artillery, HHB | Utah |
| 16th Engineer Brigade | Ohio |
| 30th Engineer Brigade (Theater), HHC | North Carolina |
| 35th Engineer Brigade (Corps), HHC | Missouri |
| 66th Aviation Brigade, HHC | Washington |
| 194th Engineer Brigade (Theater), HHC | Tennessee |
| 167th Support Command (Corps), HHC | Alabama |
| 43d Military Police Brigade, HHC | Rhode Island |
| 177th Military Police Brigade, HHC | Michigan |
| 184th Transportation Group, HHC | Mississippi |
| 142d Signal Brigade, HHC | Alabama |
| 261st Signal Brigade, HHC | Delaware |
| 228th Signal Brigade, HHC | South Carolina |
| 111th Air Defense Artillery Brigade, HHB | New Mexico |
| 263d Air Defense Artillery Brigade, HHB | South Carolina |
| 300th Military Intelligence Brigade | Utah |
| 45th Field Artillery Brigade | Oklahoma |
| 54th Field Artillery Brigade | Virginia |
| 57th Field Artillery Brigade | Wisconsin |
| 103d Field Artillery Brigade | Rhode Island |
| 113th Field Artillery Brigade | North Carolina |
| 115th Field Artillery Brigade | Wyoming |
| 130th Field Artillery Brigade | Kansas |
| 135th Field Artillery Brigade | Missouri |
| 138th Field Artillery Brigade | Kentucky |
| 142d Field Artillery Brigade | Arkansas |
| 147th Field Artillery Brigade | South Dakota |
| 151st Field Artillery Brigade | South Carolina |
| 153d Field Artillery Brigade | Arizona |
| 169th Field Artillery Brigade | Colorado |
| 196th Field Artillery Brigade | Tennessee |
| 197th Field Artillery Brigade | New Hampshire |
| 631st Field Artillery Brigade | Mississippi |

| | |
|---|---|
| 63d Aviation Group | Mississippi |
| 211th Aviation Group | Utah |
| 385th Aviation Group | Arizona |
| 449th Aviation Group | North Carolina |
| 260th MP Command | Washington, DC |
| 33d Area Support Group | Illinois |
| 404th Rear Area Operations Center | Illinois |
| 852d Rear Area Operations Center | Arizona |

Additional Guard Units

- 1 Infantry Group (Scout)
- 11 Engineer Groups, HHC
- 5 Aviation Groups, HHC
- 13 Attack Helicopter Battalions
- 1 ATS Group, HHC
- 4 Support Groups, HHC
- 8 Area Support Groups, HHC
- 5 Signal Battalions
- 1 Infantry Battalion (Mountain) (Separate)
- 1 Infantry Battalion (Light) (Separate)
- 49 Field Artillery Battalions
- 10 Air Defense Artillery Battalions
- 39 Engineer Battalions (Combat)
- 13 Signal Battalions
- 2 Special Forces Groups
- 1 Ordnance Group, HHC
- 8 Military Intelligence Battalions
- 54 State Area Commands

## Air National Guard Units
### Air Combat Command

| | |
|---|---|
| 103d Fighter Wing | Connecticut |
| 104th Fighter Wing | Massachusetts |
| 106th Rescue Wing | New York |
| 110th Fighter Wing | Michigan |
| 111th Fighter Wing | Pennsylvania |
| 114th Fighter Wing | South Dakota |
| 115th Fighter Wing | Wisconsin |
| 116th Fighter Wing | Georgia |
| 119th Fighter Wing | North Dakota |
| 120th Fighter Wing | Montana |
| 122d Fighter Wing | Indiana |
| 129th Rescue Wing | California |
| 131st Fighter Wing | Missouri |

| 132d Fighter Wing | Iowa |
| 138th Fighter Wing | Oklahoma |
| 147th Fighter Wing | Texas |
| 148th Fighter Wing | Minnesota |
| 150th Fighter Wing | New Mexico |
| 158th Fighter Wing | Vermont |
| 159th Fighter Wing | Louisiana |
| 169th Fighter Wing | South Carolina |
| 174th Fighter Wing | New York |
| 177th Fighter Wing | New Jersey |
| 180th Fighter Wing | Ohio |
| 181st Fighter Wing | Indiana |
| 183d Fighter Wing | Illinois |
| 184th Fighter Wing | Kansas |
| 185th Fighter Wing | Iowa |
| 187th Fighter Wing | Alabama |
| 188th Fighter Wing | Arkansas |
| 192d Fighter Wing | Virginia |
| 113th Wing | Maryland |
| 124th Wing | Idaho |
| 127th Wing | Michigan |
| 140th Wing | Colorado |
| 175th Wing | Maryland |

**Air Defense**

| 102d Fighter Wing | Massachusetts |
| 125th Fighter Wing | Florida |
| 142d Fighter Wing | Oregon |
| 144th Fighter Wing | California |

**Air Mobility Command**

| 105th Airlift Wing | New York |
| 109th Airlift Wing | New York |
| 118th Airlift Wing | Tennessee |
| 123d Airlift Wing | Kentucky |
| 130th Airlift Wing | West Virginia |
| 133d Airlift Wing | Minnesota |
| 136th Airlift Wing | Texas |
| 137th Airlift Wing | Oklahoma |
| 139th Airlift Wing | Missouri |
| 143d Airlift Wing | Rhode Island |
| 145th Airlift Wing | North Carolina |
| 146th Airlift Wing | California |
| 152d Airlift Wing | Nevada |

| | |
|---|---|
| 153d Airlift Wing | Wyoming |
| 156th Airlift Wing | Puerto Rico |
| 164th Airlift Wing | Tennessee |
| 165th Airlift Wing | Georgia |
| 166th Airlift Wing | Delaware |
| 167th Airlift Wing | West Virginia |
| 172d Airlift Wing | Mississippi |
| 179th Airlift Wing | Ohio |
| 182d Airlift Wing | Illinois |
| 101st Air Refueling Wing | Maine |
| 107th Air Refueling Wing | New York |
| 108th Air Refueling Wing | New Jersey |
| 117th Air Refueling Wing | Alabama |
| 121st Air Refueling Wing | Ohio |
| 126th Air Refueling Wing | Illinois |
| 128th Air Refueling Wing | Wisconsin |
| 134th Air Refueling Wing | Tennessee |
| 141st Air Refueling Wing | Washington |
| 151st Air Refueling Wing | Utah |
| 155th Air Refueling Wing | Nebraska |
| 157th Air Refueling Wing | New Hampshire |
| 161st Air Refueling Wing | Arizona |
| 163d Air Refueling Wing | California |
| 171st Air Refueling Wing | Pennsylvania |
| 186th Air Refueling Wing | Mississippi |
| 190th Air Refueling Wing | Kansas |

**Air Education and Training Command**

| | |
|---|---|
| 149th Fighter Wing | Texas |
| 162d Fighter Wing | Arizona |
| 173d Fighter Wing | Oregon |
| 178th Fighter Wing | Ohio |
| 189th Airlift Wing | Arkansas |

**Pacific Air Forces**

| | |
|---|---|
| 154th Wing | Hawaii |
| 168th Air Refueling Wing | Alaska |
| 176th Wing | Alaska |

**Special Operations Command**

| | |
|---|---|
| 193d Special Operations Wing | Pennsylvania |

* Appendix based on a table in the *2001 National Guard Almanac*
published by Uniformed Services Almanac, Inc.

# BIBLIOGRAPHY

Cooper, Jerry. *The Militia and the National Guard in America Since Colonial Times: A Research Guide.* Westport, Conn.: Greenwood Press, 1993.

Derthick, Martha. *The National Guard in Politics.* Cambridge, Mass.: Harvard University Press, 1965.

Doubler, Michael D. *I Am the Guard: A History of the Army National Guard, 1636–2000.* Washington, D.C.: Office of the Director, Army National Guard, 2001.

Gordon, Martin K. *Imprint on the Nation: Stories Reflecting the National Guard's Impact on a Changing Nation.* Manhattan, Kans.: Sunflower University Press, 1983.

Gross, Charles J. *The Air National Guard and the American Military Tradition.* Washington, D.C.: National Guard Bureau, Historical Services Division, 1995.

———. *Prelude to the Total Force: The Air National Guard, 1943–1946.* Washington, D.C.: Office of Air Force History, 1985.

Hill, Jim Dan. *The Minute Man in Peace and War: A History of the National Guard.* Harrisburg, Penn.: Stackpole Books, 1964.

Mahon, John K. *History of the Militia and National Guard.* New York: Macmillan, 1983.

Millett, Allan R., and Peter Maslowski. *For the Common Defense: A Military History of the United States of America.* New York: The Free Press, 1984.

National Guard Association of the United States. *The Nation's National Guard.* Buffalo, N.Y.: Baker, Jones, Hausauer, Inc., 1954.

Riker, William H. *Soldiers of the States.* New York: Arno Press, 1979.

# INDEX

Numbers in *italics* refer to photographs and illustrations.

Arnold, Benedict, *11*, 13
Arnold, Henry H., 135
Artillery Corps, 39
Ashcroft, John, *122*
Assize of Arms, 1
atomic bombs, 97

B-1B bombers, *162*
B-26 "Invaders," *136*
Bacon, Francis, *5*
Baghdad, 135, 138
Bagram Air Base, *134*
Baker, Addison, *90*
Balkans, 130, *131*, 162–63, *163*, *164*
balloons, observation, *59*
Battalion of National Guards, 24–25
Battery A, 108th Field Artillery, 28th Division, *62*
Battery B, 140th Field Artillery, 39th Division, *67*
Battery C, 130th Field Artillery, 35th Division, *64*
Battery D, 129th Field Artillery, 35th Division, *59*
Battery F, 111th Field Artillery, 29th Division, *60*
Battle of Bennington, 14
Battle of Cerro Gordo, 30
Battle of the Thames, 21, *21*
"Battling Bastards of Bataan," 78, *79*
Beightler, Robert S., 97
Berkeley, Sir William, *5*
Berlin Crisis
    role of Air National Guard, 139–41
    role of Army National Guard, 109–10
bin Laden, Osama, 134
Blackhawk helicopters, *119*
Bladensburg Races, 21
Blazing Trails, 121
Bleckley, Erwin B., 66, *66*

blockhouses, 6, *6*
Blum, H. Steven, 140, *140*
Bolling, Raynal C., 65--66, *66*
Boonesborough Fort, *12*
Border Patrol, 140–41, 178
border protection, 58–59, 133
Boston, siege of, 10
Boston City Greys, *27*
Boston Lancers, *24*
Bouger, Michael, *130*
Bowling Green Guard, *44*
Breed's Hill, 10
bridges, *121*
British Regulars, 7–8, 15, 21–22
Brittain, William, *34*
Brown, John, 33
Buena Vista, battle of, 29
Buna (New Guinea), 81
Bunker Hill, battle of, 10–11
Burnside, Ambrose E., *41*
Bush, George H. W., 122, 125, *164*
Bush, George W. , 140, 172, *173*
Butterfield, Daniel, *41*

C-5 "Galaxies," *156*
C-45A cargo carriers, *80*
C-47 "Gooney Birds," *138*
C-97 "Stratocruisers," 143
C-97 "Stratofreighters," *145*
C-121 "Super Constellations," 143, *145*
C-124 "Globemasters," *151*
C-130 "Hercules," 111, *151*, *159*, *175*
C-141 "Starlifters," *156*, 157
Callison, Ernest, *96*
Camp Kearny, *60*
Camp MacArthur, *60*
Camp MacKenzie, *47*
Camp McClellan, *60*
Camp Perry, *55*
Camp Riley, *55*
Camp Ripley, *107*
Camp Thompson, *25*, *27*

Camp Wheeler, *61*
Castillo de San Marcos, *2*
Central America, 121
Cerro Gordo, battle of, *30*
CH-47 helicopters, *118*
Charlestown Peninsula, occupation of, 10
Chatham Artillery, *44*
Cheatham, Benjamin, *40*
Cheyenne Guard, *43*
Chickasaw Guards, *46*
"Chicken Little," *90*
Childers, Ernest, *84*
China-Burma-India Theater, 96
Chinook helicopters, *118*
Christianity, and Native Americans, 3
civil disobedience, 8
civil unrest, 112–14, 126, *149*
Civil War, 33–41
Clay, Henry, Jr., *29*
Clinch Rifles, *38*
Clinton, William J., 125
coastal defense, 56
Coast Artillery, 56
Cold War, missions, 105, 107–8
*Colonel Johnson's Mounted Men Charging a Party of British and Indians at Moravian Town*, 21
colonial wars, 7
Company A, 1st Mississippi Infantry, *45*
Company A, 1st Regiment, Virginia Volunteers, *32*
Company A, 3d Battalion, Kentucky State Guard, *44*
Company A, 5th Georgia Infantry, *38*
Company A, Mercer Brigade, New Jersey State Militia, *36*
Company B, 1st North Dakota Volunteer Infantry, *51*
Company B, 117th Infantry, 30th Infantry Division, *63*

# UNITS AND DIVISIONS

# ABOUT THE AUTHORS

**Col. Michael D. Doubler** (Ret.) served twenty-three years on active duty as a Regular Army and full-time Army National Guard officer. He is a graduate of the U.S. Military Academy and holds a doctorate degree in military history from the Ohio State University. He is the author of *I Am the Guard: A History of the Army National Guard, 1636–2000,* the Army National Guard's first official history. His previous works include the award-winning *Closing With the Enemy: How GIs Fought the War in Europe, 1944–1945.* Colonel Doubler is a member of the Board of Directors of the National Guard Educational Foundation and a frequent commentator on the *History Channel.*

**CW2 John W. Listman Jr.,** (Ret.) served twenty-two years of combined active duty and Army National Guard service. He was a medic in Vietnam (1971–72) and was the command historian of the Virginia Army National Guard for eighteen years. Chief Listman worked eight years as curator of collections of the museum operated by the National Guard Educational Foundation. He is coauthor of *The Tradition Continues: A History of the Virginia National Guard, 1607–1985.* And he has had numerous articles published in *National Guard* magazine covering various topics in National Guard history.